A stomach t
empty desp

food.
-- Horace

When thou hast eaten and art full, then thou shalt bless
the LORD thy God for the good land which he hath
given thee. Deuteronomy 8:10

Appetizers & Soups

Easy Potato Soup

Faye Chapman, Milton, WV

16 oz. frozen hash brown potatoes	1 can cream of celery soup
1 c. chopped onions	1 can cream of chicken soup
1 14 1/2 oz. chicken broth	2 c. milk
2 c. water	8 oz. cheddar cheese

Combine first four ingredients. Bring to boil. Cover, reduce heat and simmer thirty minutes. Stir in soups, milk, and cheese. Heat thoroughly.

Cream of Broccoli Soup

Mary Fellure, Milton, FL

1 pkg. frozen broccoli cuts	1/2 c. chopped onion (sauté in butter)
1 c. half and half	1 c. milk
1 can potato soup	1/2 stick butter
1 can celery soup	(Season to taste)

Combine all ingredients, bring to boil and then lower heat. Cook about 1/2 hour until thickened.

Broccoli Cheese Soup

Selected

3 or 4 pkgs. chopped broccoli	4 cans cheddar cheese soup
4 cans chicken stock	2 cans evaporated milk
1 medium onion, chopped	

Mix broccoli, chicken stock and onion. Cook until broccoli is done. Add cheddar cheese soup, blending well. Add evaporated milk. Simmer until well blended.

Anything Dip

Selected

1/2 c. mayonnaise	Season to taste
1/4 c. ketchup	Dash of red pepper (optional)

Mix ingredients thoroughly.

Bean Soup
Elsie Gilkerson, Milton, FL

1 lb. dry navy beans	Salt & pepper to taste
2 quarts water	1/2 c. chopped celery leaves
1 lb. meaty ham bone or pieces	1 medium onion, chopped

Combine all ingredients and cook over low heat for approximately 1 1/2 to 2 hours. Makes 2 1/2 quarts.

Vegetable Soup
Elsie Gilkerson, Milton, FL

2 lbs. cubed beef	1 can of corn
1 - 48 oz. can of tomato juice	1 can of peas or green beans
3 or 4 potatoes, cubed	Half of a cabbage head, shredded
1 medium onion, chopped	2 carrots, sliced

Cook meat until tender. Leaving about 1 to 2 c. of meat broth, add the remaining ingredients and cook over low heat for approximately 1 hour or until vegetables are tender.

Potato Cheese Soup
Selected

3 medium potatoes, peeled and quartered	3 c. milk
1 small onion, finely chopped	3 Tbs. butter
1 c. water	2 Tbs. all purpose flour
1 tsp. salt	2 Tbs. minced fresh parsley
	1 c. shredded Swiss cheese

In a saucepan bring potatoes, onion, water and salt to boil. Reduce heat, cover and simmer until potatoes are tender. Do not drain. Mash slightly, stir in milk. In a small bowl, blend butter, flour, parsley and pepper; stir into potato mixture. Cook and stir over medium heat until thickened and bubbly. Remove from heat; add cheese and stir until melted.

Chicken Soup

Maddy Ray, Phoenix, AZ

1 whole chicken
1 can peas
1 can corn
1 can carrots

1 can cream of chicken soup
Salt & pepper to taste
3 lg. potatoes, cut up

Boil chicken until cooked and debone. Using stock from chicken, add remaining ingredients. Season to take. Cook until potatoes are tender.

Chicken Noodle Soup

Selected

1 whole chicken
1 stalk celery, diced
1 lg. potato, diced
1 lg. onion, diced

1 carrot diced
Egg noodles-App. 2 c.
Salt & pepper to taste

Boil chicken; debone. In broth place the vegetables and cook. Return chicken to broth and cook until carrots are tender. Add noodles and cook until done.

Hamburger Soup

Elsie Gilkerson, Milton, FL

1/2 lb. lean ground beef
1/2 c. chopped onion
2 ribs celery, diced
1/2 c. fresh mushrooms
6 c. no salt tomatoes

1 tsp. dill weed
1/4 tsp. celery salt
1 lg. carrot, thinly sliced
2 or 3 potatoes, peeled and cubed
1 tsp. basil

In a large pot, brown ground beef with onion, celery and mushrooms. Drain off any fat from meat. Add all remaining ingredients to the pot and bring to a boil. Reduce heat to a simmer for 20 minutes or until carrots and potatoes are tender.

Tomato Soup
Selected

2 c. crushed canned tomatoes
1/2 tsp. baking soda

2 c. milk
2 tsp. margarine

In a large heavy saucepan, heat tomatoes until boiling. Remove from heat; add remaining ingredients. Return to heat and cook on medium until butter is melted and the soup is heated thoroughly.

Cream of Tomato Soup
Selected

1 can diced tomatoes,
  undrained (28 oz.)
1 c. chicken broth
1/4 c. butter or margarine

2 Tbs. sugar
1 Tbs. chopped onion
2 Tbs. cream

In a saucepan, combine the first 5 ingredients. Cover and simmer for 1 hour. Heat cream in the top of a double boiler over simmering water; add to the tomato mixture just before serving. Yields 8 servings.

Mushroom & Potato Chowder
Selected

1/2 c. onions, chopped
1/4 c. margarine
2 Tbs. all purpose flour
1 tsp. salt
1/2 tsp. pepper
3 c. water

1 lb. fresh mushrooms, sliced
1 c. celery, chopped
1 c. peeled potatoes, diced
1/2 c. carrots
1 c. light cream
1/4 c. Parmesan cheese, grated

In a large saucepan, sauté onions in butter until tender. Add flour, salt and pepper; stir to make a smooth paste. Gradually add water, stirring constantly. Bring to a boil; cook and stir for one minute. Add the mushrooms, celery, potatoes and carrots. Reduce heat, cover and simmer for 30 minutes or until vegetables are tender. Add cream and Parmesan cheese, heating through. 4 - 6 servings.

Cheese Balls
Norma Moore, Tyro, NC

1 package cream cheese (8 oz.)
1 package chipped ham or beef
2 Tbs. Worcestershire sauce
1 small onion, chopped fine
1/2 c. chopped pecans

Let cream cheese soften at room temperature. Chop nuts very fine; set aside. Mix together all ingredients, except nuts. Form into ball or long roll. Roll cheese ball in nuts on waxed paper. Keep in refrigerator.

Cheese Log
Selected

16 oz. cream cheese, softened
16 oz. sharp cheddar cheese, shredded
1 small onion, chopped extra fine
1 small jar pimento, drained & chopped
2 Tbs. green pepper, chopped

Mix together. Makes 2 logs. Roll in chopped pecans. Chill until set.

Cranberry Log
Tanya Morris, San Antonio, TX

2 8 oz. cream cheese, softened
3 Tbs. cinnamon
1/2 c. confectioners sugar
1 c. raisins
1 pkg. fresh cranberries
1 1/2 c. sugar
1 1/2 c. water

Beat together cream cheese and confectioners sugar. Cook until thickened berries and all the other ingredients until berries have popped. Cool, spoon over log and serve with crackers.

Fruit Dip
Selected

8 oz. cream cheese, softened
7 oz. jar marshmallow cream

Combine the ingredients and mix until well blended.

Cranberry Crunch

Norma Moore, Tyro, NC

1 1/2 c. uncooked oats
1/2 c. all purpose flour
3/4 c. brown sugar

1/3 c. margarine
1 can (16 oz.) cranberry sauce

Preheat oven to 350°. In a bowl mix together oats, flour, and brown sugar.
Cut in butter until crumbly. Press half of the mixture into a 8 inch square
baking dish. Spread on cranberry sauce. Top with remaining crumb mixture.
Bake 45 minutes. Serve warm with ice cream. Makes 9 servings.

Kenya Peanuts

Selected

2 c. raw peanuts
1 c. sugar

1/2 c. water

Combine and cook until moisture is gone. (Watch carefully)
Spread on cookie sheet and bake at 325° for 20 minutes.

Vegetable Dip

Kate Cravatt, Brewton, AL

16 oz. sour cream
16 oz. mayonnaise
2 Tbs. dill seed

2 Tbs. Accent
1 small onion, chopped finely

Mix all ingredients well.

Crab Dip

Doris Twiddy, Kinston, NC

2 - 8 oz. pkgs. cream cheese
1 to 2 lbs. crab meat
Seasoning salt to taste

Garlic powder, optional
1 tsp. lemon juice

Roll ingredients into ball and let chill.

Cranberry-Orange Appetizer

Chris Perrine, Milton, FL

6 c. cranberry juice
1 c. frozen orange juice
  (undiluted)

1 1/4 c. pineapple juice
3 c. ice water
3 Tbs. lemon juice

Mix ingredients in order given. Chill well and serve.

Dairy Delicious Dip

Selected

8 oz. pkg. cream cheese, softened
1/2 c. sour cream
1/4 c. sugar

1/4 c. brown sugar
1 to 2 Tbs. maple syrup

In a small mixing bowl, combine cream cheese, sour cream, sugars and syrup; beat until smooth. Chill. Serve with fresh fruit.

Mexican Dip

Selected

1 lb. ground beef
1 onion, chopped
1 green pepper, chopped
3 Tbs. chili powder

1 can tomato soup
1 can golden mushroom soup
1 lb. Velveeta cheese (Mexican mild)
8 oz. longhorn cheese

Brown ground beef with onion and green pepper and drain. Add remaining ingredients and simmer in crock pot until cheese is melted. Serve with Nacho chips.

Fruit Dip

Selected

8 oz. cream cheese
2/3 c. confectioners sugar

4 oz. sour cream
1 1/2 tsp. vanilla

Blend all ingredients in a blender until smooth and creamy. Let stand about a half hour before serving.

Raw Vegetable Dip
Selected

1 pt. sour cream
1 pt. mayonnaise
1 pkg. dry onion soup mix

1 pkg. Hidden Valley Ranch party mix
Garlic powder to taste

Mix all ingredients and let stand in refrigerator overnight.

Low Calorie Dip
Selected

1 lg. container cottage cheese
1 can small shrimp, drained
1/4 tsp. pepper

Dash salt
Dash of garlic powder
Dash of paprika

Put above ingredients into blender and process until creamy. Serve cold with any fresh vegetables

Nacho Dip
Selected

1 lb. sausage
1 lb. hamburger
1 lb. cheese (melted)

1 can cream of mushroom soup
1 can of Ro-tel tomatoes

Brown sausage and hamburger meat. Drain fat. Add melted cheese, mushroom soup and Ro-tel tomatoes. Serve with Nacho chips.

Guacamole Dip
Selected

2 medium avocados,
   seeded and peeled
1 thin slice of small onion
1 Tbs. lemon juice

1/2 tsp. salt
1 clove garlic

In a blender combine avocados, onion, lemon juice, garlic and salt. Blend till smooth. Place in a serving bowl, cover and chill. Serve with fresh vegetables.

Corn Beef Cheese Ball
Selected

3 8 oz. pkgs. cream cheese
3 pkgs. chipped corn beef
2 bunches green onions, chopped

1 Tbs. Worcestershire sauce
Dash of garlic powder
Dash of seasoned salt

Let cheese reach room temperature. Chop corned beef, saving some for use on outside of ball. Mix all ingredients and shape into ball. Pat extra corned beef onto outside of ball. Recipe makes one large cheese ball or 2 -3 smaller ones and may be frozen for later use.

Hot Chili Dip
Selected

1 lb. ground beef
2 medium onions, chopped
2 cans chili beef soup (11 1/4 oz.)
2 cans green chilies &
   tomatoes (10 oz.)

1 can refried beans (15 oz.)
1/4 lb. grated cheese
12 green olives, sliced
4 green onions, sliced
Salt & pepper to taste

Brown beef and onions in skillet, season to taste. Place beef and onions in slow cooker, add soup, chilies, tomatoes and beans. Stir. Cover and cook 2 hours on high setting. When ready to serve, top with cheese, olives and green onions. Serves 25.

Ham Pinwheels
Donna Lisenbee, Boaz, AL

2 cans (4 1/2 oz.) deviled ham
1 c. (3 - 4 oz.) mushrooms,
   drained & minced
1/4 c. minced dill pickle

1 Tbs. prepared mustard
2 Tbs. parsley
2 pkg. crescent dinner rolls

Blend all ingredients in bowl except rolls. Spread crescent rolls with mixture and roll up, starting from small end and pinch to seal. Cut into 8 slices. Place on large cookie sheet and bake until lightly browned. Serve hot or cold.

Pimento Cheese Spread
Selected

2 c. shredded cheddar cheese
3 Tbs. mayonnaise
1 (4 oz.) can chopped grn. chilies

1/8 tsp. garlic powder
1/8 tsp. cayenne pepper
1 (2 oz.) jar diced pimentos, undrained

Combine all ingredients. Cover and refrigerate.

Cheese Pennies
Donna Lisenbee, Boaz, AL

1/3 c. mayonnaise
1/2 lb. grated cheddar cheese

1 c. flour
1 Tbs. onion soup mix

Combine all ingredients until dough forms. Separate into 2 rolls. Wrap separately in waxed paper and chill one hour until firm. Slice pennies 1/2 inch thick. Bake on ungreased cookie sheet 8 to 10 minutes at 400⁰ .

BBQ Cups
Donna Lisenbee, Boaz, AL

1 can of biscuits
1 lb. hamburger meat,
   cooked & drained

BBQ sauce

Press biscuits into muffin tins, forming a bowl shape with the dough. Spoon the browned hamburger into biscuit dough adding enough sauce to coat meat. Bake according to biscuit directions.

White Trash
Kathy DeFoor, Godley, TX

3 c. Honeycomb cereal
2 c. Alphabet cereal
2 c. miniature marshmallows
1 c. peanuts

1 c. pecans
2 c. pretzels
1 whole pkg. white bark

Melt white bark and pour over mixture; spread out and let dry.

Hot Dip
Nancy Schrader, San Antonio, TX

3 16 oz. can tomatoes,
   drained and chopped
1 Tbs. minced onion

1 Tbs. garlic powder
Dash of salt
1 jalapeño pepper, chopped

Mix ingredients and heat thoroughly. Serve while hot.

Party Mix
Mary Fellure, Milton, FL

1/4 c. melted margarine
1/2 tsp. Worcestershire sauce
1/4 tsp. celery salt
1/4 tsp. garlic salt
1 1/2 c. Kix cereal

1 c. Cheerios cereal
2 c. small cheese crackers
1 c. thin pretzel sticks
1/2 lb. mixed nuts
1 pkg. corn chips (app. 4 oz.)

Heat oven to 250^0. Blend margarine and seasonings. Place all other ingredients in 13 x 9 pan. Pour butter mixture over and stir. Bake 1 hour, stirring every 15 minutes.

Party Mints
Selected

1 stick margarine, softened
1 box confectioners sugar
5 drops oil of peppermint,
  or other if desired

1 Tbs. water
Coloring your choice

Cream together all ingredients with fork. Blend with hands. Press in mold.

Sugar Baked Pecans
Selected

2 1/2 c. pecan halves
1 egg white, beaten stiff

1 c. light brown sugar
1 tsp. vanilla

Beat egg white and fold sugar and vanilla into it. Dip pecans in mixture and place nuts on cookie sheet, sprayed with cooking spray. Bake 30 minutes at 250^0. Turn stove off and let nuts set 30 more minutes in oven.
Note: When placing nuts on baking sheet, do not let them touch.

11

Give us this day our daily bread

--Matthew 6:11

Now them that are such we command and exhort by our Lord Jesus Christ, that with quietness they work, and eat their own bread. 2 Thessalonians 3:12

Mom's Buttermilk Biscuits
Selected

2 c. all-purpose flour
2 tsp. baking powder
1/2 tsp. baking soda

1/2 tsp. salt
1/4 c. shortening
3/4 c. buttermilk

In a bowl, combine the flour, baking powder, baking soda and salt; cut in shortening until the mixture resembles coarse crumbs. Stir in buttermilk and knead dough gently. Roll out to 1/2 inch thickness. Cut with a 2 1/2 inch biscuit cutter and place on a lightly greased baking sheet. Bake at 450^0 for 10-15 minutes or until golden brown.

Potato Chive Bread
Selected

1 pkg. active dry yeast
1/4 c. warm milk
4 c. all-purpose flour
1 tsp. salt

2 c. boiled, mashed potatoes
1/2 c. warm milk
1/2 c. warm water
3 Tbs. chopped chives

In small bowl, sprinkle yeast over 1/4 c. warm milk. Stir until dissolved. Let stand 15 minutes. In a large bowl, combine flour and salt. Cut in mashed potatoes with a pastry blender. Stir in yeast mixture. Gradually stir in remaining milk and water. Turn out on a floured surface. Knead dough until smooth and elastic, about eight minutes. Knead in chives. Turn dough into buttered bowl. Cover with a tea towel and let rise in a warm place 1 1/2 hours until double in bulk. Punch dough down. Shape into a loaf. Place in buttered 9 x 5 x 3 loaf pan. Cover with damp cloth; let rise 30 more minutes. Bake in 375^0 oven for 40 - 50 minutes until loaf sounds hollow when thumped.

Dumplings
Mary Fellure, Milton, FL

2 c. flour (self-rising)
1 egg

1/4 c. shortening
Hot water to mix

Mix ingredients to form ball, kneading flour to make the right consistency desired. Roll out as thin as possible; cut into strips and place in boiling broth.

Chew Bread
Betty Thomas, Greenville, NC

1 box of light brown sugar
3 eggs
2 c. self-rising flour

1 stick margarine
1 c. chopped pecans

Melt margarine and add to other ingredients. Bake in a greased pan at 350⁰ for 30 minutes.

Cornbread Dressing
Geraldine Chapman, Brunswick, GA

Cornbread
Light Bread
Swanson Chicken Broth
3 eggs

1/2 c. milk
1 medium onion, chopped
1 tsp. poultry seasoning
Salt & pepper to taste

Cook cornbread, cool and crumble. Also crumble light bread, enough to make 2 cups. Add 1 large or 3 small cans broth. Also add chicken broth as needed. Add remaining ingredients and bake in greased baking dish at 350⁰ for 30 to 40 minutes.

Sweet Cornbread
Selected

1 c. cornmeal
1 1/2 c. flour
4 tsp. baking powder
1/2 tsp. salt

1 1/2 c. milk
1 egg, beaten
1/4 c. oil
1/2 c. sugar

Preheat oven to 400⁰. Mix dry ingredients. Add the rest of the ingredients. A few lumps will remain in the batter. Pour into greased 8" pan and bake for 25 minutes or until golden brown.

14

Cornbread
Mary Fellure, Milton, FL

1 c. self-rising corn meal
1 c. self-rising flour
1 egg, beaten

1/2 to 3/4 c. buttermilk (may need
    some water)

Heat shortening in small iron skillet. Drain off excess shortening and pour batter into pan. Bake at 350⁰ to 375⁰ degrees for 20 minutes, then turn oven on broil and brown the top.

North Carolina's Best Cornbread
Marie St. John, Burlington, NC

2 eggs, beaten
1 small can of creamed corn
1/3 c. oil
1 c. sour cream

1 c. plus 2 Tbs. plain cornmeal
1 1/2 tsp. salt
3 tsp. baking powder

Add all ingredients to beaten eggs and beat on slow speed of mixer until blended. Pour into well greased pan. Bake at 375⁰ for 40 to 50 minutes. Note: A very soft, moist cornbread.

Corn Pone
Selected

5 or 6 c. corn meal
1 c. flour
1/2 c. sugar
1 tsp. soda

5 c. warm water
1 1/2 c. buttermilk
1 egg
2 tsp. baking powder

Grease baking pan and mix all ingredients. Bake at 350⁰ for 1 hour or until golden brown.

Raisin-Walnut Bread

Betty Thomas, Greenville, NC

1 1/4 c. raisins	1 c. sugar
1 1/4 c. water	1 tsp. vanilla extract
1 1/2 tsp. baking soda	2 c. unsifted all-purpose flour
3 Tbs. vegetable oil	1/2 tsp. salt
2 eggs	1 c. chopped walnuts

In small saucepan, bring raisins, water, baking soda and vegetable oil to a boil. Remove from heat and set aside to cool in large bowl. Use mixer and beat the eggs, sugar and vanilla until blended. Add cooled raisin mixture alternately with flour and salt to egg-sugar mixture. Stir until well mixed. You can bake in loaf pans in 350⁰ oven for approximately 45 minutes or until golden brown.

Quick Pone

Lisa Bailes, Summersville, WV

2 c. meal	1/2 c. hot water
3/4 c. flour	1/2 tsp. baking soda
1 1/2 tsp. salt	1 egg
1/2 c. sugar	1/2 c. buttermilk
1 tsp. baking powder	

Blend meal, flour, salt, sugar, and baking powder. Add water, egg, buttermilk and soda. Pour into greased pan. Bake at 400⁰ for 1 hour.

Potato Rolls

Gladys Coker, New Caney, TX

1 1/2 c. warm water	1 stick butter
2 pkgs. yeast	1 egg
1 c. mashed potatoes	1 tsp. salt
1/2 c. sugar	6 or 7 c. flour

Dissolve yeast in warm water. Mix in all ingredients, except flour. Add flour one cup at a time. Knead and let rise (covered) in warm place. Knead again and form rolls. Let rise until double. Bake at 350⁰ until done.

Fried Bread

Toni Farris, Gallup, NM

2 c. flour
1/4 c. powdered milk (opt.)
1 tsp. salt

3 tsp. baking powder
Enough warm water to make soft dough

Knead dough. Let rise 30 minutes. Pinch off in small portions to make round balls and roll out as thin as possible. Fry in hot grease for 3 seconds on each side.
Note: Use as taco shell.

Monti's Roman Bread

Selected

1 cake yeast
1 Tbs. sugar
1 1/2 c. lukewarm water
4 c. flour

1/2 c. finely chopped onion
1 tsp. salt
Dried rosemary
Oil & salt as needed

Add sugar and yeast to lukewarm water and stir to dissolve yeast. Add flour, salt and onion. Knead until smooth. Place dough in an oiled bowl and let rise until doubled in size; punch it down. Flatten out dough on oiled cookie sheet to about an inch thick. Oil the top of the dough. Let rise again until doubled. Sprinkle with salt and dried rosemary. Bake at 400° for 20 to 25 minutes. Serve hot.

Dumplings

Selected

1 1/2 c. flour
1/4 c. Crisco
1/2 tsp. salt

1/4 c. milk
1 egg

Cut flour, Crisco, and salt in mixing bowl until it resembles cornmeal. Add milk and egg. Roll out on floured board and cut into strips. Let dry for 30 minutes before placing in broth. Cook for 20 minutes without taking lid off.

Cheese Bread
Selected

1 pkg. dry yeast
1/4 c. warm water
1 c. sour cream
1 egg, beaten
2 Tbs. sugar

1 tsp. salt
2 1/2 c. all-purpose flour
1 c. shredded cheddar cheese
1/2 tsp. pepper

Dissolve yeast in water. Add the sour cream, egg, sugar, salt and 2/3 c. flour; beat until smooth. Stir in enough remaining flour to form a soft dough. It will be sticky. Fold in cheese and pepper. Divide in half. Place in two greased containers and let rise until doubled in size. Bake at 350⁰ for 45 to 50 minutes. Yields 2 loaves.

Refrigerator Rolls
Maddy Ray, Tempe, AZ

1 pkg. yeast
1/2 c. sugar
1 1/2 tsp. salt
1 stick oleo

2 c. warm water
3 eggs
7 c. flour

Dissolve yeast, salt & sugar in water; add oleo, eggs and flour. Make into rolls and bake at 350⁰ for 15 - 20 minutes.
Note: This can also be refrigerated and used within 5 or 6 days.

Hot Rolls
Lisa Bailes, Summersville, WV

2 pkg. yeast (rapid-rise)
2 c. warm water
1/2 c. to 3/4 c. sugar
1/3 c. oil

1 tsp. salt
1 egg
6 to 7 c. flour

Mix yeast and water; then add other ingredients. Let rise at least 2 hours. Then make into rolls and let rise another half hour. Bake at 400⁰ for 20 to 30 minutes.

Egg Bread
Selected

2 pkg. dry yeast	2 eggs, beaten
1/2 c. warm water	1/4 c. butter, softened
1 1/2 c. warm milk	7 - 7 1/2 c. all purpose flour
1/4 c. sugar	1 egg yolk
1 Tbs. salt	2 Tbs. water

Dissolve yeast in water. Add milk, sugar, salt, eggs, butter and 3 1/2 c. flour. Mix well. Stir in enough remaining flour to form a soft dough. On a floured surface, knead until smooth and elastic, about six minutes. Place in greased bowl; turn to grease top. Cover and let rise in a warm place until doubled in size, app. 2 hours. Punch down; cover and let rise until almost doubled again, about 30 minutes. Divide into six sections. On a floured surface, shape each into a 14 inch rope. For each loaf, braid three ropes together on a greased baking sheet, pinch ends to seal. Cover and let rise until doubled, about 1 hour. Beat egg yolks and water, brush over loaves. Bake at 375^0 for 30 to 35 minutes. Yields 2 loaves.

Bread Pudding
Selected

2 c. milk	3 slices of bread
3 eggs	Nutmeg
1/2 c. sugar	

Mix eggs and sugar and beat; add milk. Cut bread in pieces and put in baking dish. Pour the milk mixture over the bread. Sprinkle nutmeg over the top. Bake at 350^0 for 30 minutes.

Sour Cream Cornbread
Beulah Potts, Milton, FL

1 can cream style corn	1/2 c. oil
1 c. sour cream	2 eggs
1 1/2 c. self-rising meal	

Mix ingredients thoroughly and pour into hot greased large skillet. Bake 30 minutes at 400^0.

Honey Whole Wheat Bread
Selected

3 c. water	1/2 c. nonfat dry milk powder
1/4 c. honey	2 tsp. salt
2 Tbs. oil	2 pkg. active dry yeast
5 c. whole wheat flour	3 to 3 1/2 c. all-purpose flour

Heat water, honey and oil in saucepan. Cool to lukewarm. Combine 3 c. whole wheat flour, powdered milk, salt and yeast in bowl. Beat in liquid on low speed about 2 minutes. Beat in remaining whole wheat flour. Mix in enough all-purpose flour to make dough soft. Knead on floured surface until smooth and elastic, about 10 minutes. Add flour to prevent sticking. Place in greased bowl, turning it to coat. Cover and let rise 50 minutes. Punch down. Divide in half. Knead a little more and place in two greased loaf pans. Cover and let rise 45 more minutes or until doubled in size. Bake in preheated oven at 375^0 for 40 minutes.

Three Hour Rolls
Selected

2 pkgs. yeast	2 tsp. salt
2 c. warm water	2 Tbs. oil
2 Tbs. sugar	5 c. all purpose flour

Dissolve yeast in warm water. Add sugar, salt and oil. Gradually add flour, stirring well. Let rise for 1 1/2 hours; punch down. Make rolls and put in greased pan. Let rise 1 1/2 hours. Bake at 350^0 until golden brown.

Mexican Cornbread
Mary Fellure, Milton, FL

1 c. cornmeal	2 tsp. diced hot pepper
1/2 tsp. salt	1 c. buttermilk
1/2 tsp. soda	8 oz. can of corn (whole kernel)
1/3 c. melted butter	2 eggs beaten
1 c. shredded cheddar cheese	Chopped onion (optional)

Stir together until well mixed. Bake in iron skillet 375^0 for 40 minutes or until golden brown.

Dinner Rolls

Vicki Richburg, Six Mile, SC

2 3/4 to 3 1/4 c. unsifted flour
1/4 c. sugar
1/2 tsp. salt
1 pkg. yeast

5 Tbs. softened oleo
2/3 c. very hot tap water
1 egg, room temp.

In large bowl thoroughly mix 3/4 c. flour, sugar, salt and undissolved yeast. Add softened oleo. Gradually add very hot water to dry ingredients and beat 2 minutes at medium speed, scraping bowl. Add egg and 1/2 c. flour or enough to make thick batter. Beat at high speed 2 minutes. Add enough flour to make soft dough. Turn out and knead 8 to 10 minutes. Place in greased bowl turning to grease top. Let rise until doubled in size, about 1 hour. Punch down and make into rolls. Bake at 350^0 about 10 minutes or until golden brown.

Angel Biscuits

Mary Fellure, Milton, FL

1 package of yeast
2 Tbs. lukewarm water
2 c. self rising flour
1/4 tsp. baking soda

2 Tbs. sugar
1/2 c. shortening
3/4 c. buttermilk

Dissolve yeast in lukewarm water and let set for five minutes in mixing bowl. Mix flour, soda, and sugar together. Add flour mixture, shortening and buttermilk to the yeast, stirring with a fork or use hands to mix well. Roll in flour and cut with biscuit cutter or roll them by hand. Bake at 400^0, approximately 10 to 12 minutes.

Biscuits

Selected

4 c. of Bisquick mix
1 c. sour cream

1/3 - 1/2 c. club soda

Mix Bisquick, sour cream and club soda until it forms a soft ball. Roll out into flour, knead 3 or 4 times and cut out biscuits. Place on buttered pan and bake at 425^0 for 12-15 minutes. Brush with butter when done.

21

Sour Dough Biscuits
Selected

1 pkg. dry yeast	1/2 c. sugar
1 c. warm water	1/2 c. shortening
6 c. self-rising flour	2 c. buttermilk

Dissolve yeast in warm water. Mix dry ingredients together. Cut in shortening. Add milk and yeast. Mix well. Cover and refrigerate until cold. Roll out on floured surface and cut out. Bake at 425⁰ for 15 minutes.

Jellied Biscuits
Selected

2 c. all purpose flour	1/2 tsp. cream of tartar
4 tsp. baking powder	1/2 c. shortening
2 tsp. sugar	3/4 c. milk
1/2 tsp. salt	1/3 c. jelly

In a bowl, combine flour, baking powder, sugar, salt and cream of tartar. Cut in shortening until the mixture resembles coarse crumbs. Add milk; stir quickly with a fork until mixed. Drop by rounded tablespoonful onto a greased baking sheet. Make a deep thumbprint in tops. Fill each with one teaspoon of jelly. Bake at 450⁰ for 10-12 minutes or until biscuits are browned. Yields about 1 dozen.

Zucchini Bread
Madeline Darnell, Sulphur, LA

1/2 c. raisins	1 tsp. salt
2 c. unpeeled, grated zucchini	1 tsp. soda
2 c. sugar	3 tsp. cinnamon
1 c. oil	1/2 c. chopped nuts
3 c. flour	3 eggs
3 tsp. vanilla	1/2 tsp. baking powder

Mix all ingredients together. Bake in two loaf pans at 350⁰ for 1 hour or until done.

Bread Pudding
Elsie Gilkerson, Milton, FL

1/2 to 3/4 loaf of French bread	8 eggs
1 stick margarine	5 c. milk
2 c. sugar .	

Mix butter, sugar, eggs and milk; pour over bread and bake until brown at 350⁰. (Place baking pan in a pan of water and bake with the effect of a double boiler.)

Topping:

2 sticks butter	1 tsp. vanilla
2 eggs (well beaten)	Confectioners sugar

Mix ingredients using the confectioners sugar to get the consistency you desire. Spread on pudding and serve warm.

Mayonnaise Biscuits
Mary Jackson, Lexington, NC

1 c. self-rising flour	1/2 c. milk
2 Tbs. mayonnaise	

Mix all ingredients and spoon into muffin pan. Bake at 425⁰ until brown.

Ribbon Nut Bread
Madeline Darnell, Sulphur, LA

8 oz. cream cheese, softened	1 tsp. soda
1/3 c. butter	1/2 tsp. salt
1 egg	1/2 c. oil
1/3 c. sugar	1/2 c. milk
1/3 c. brown sugar	2 eggs
2 c. flour	1 c. nuts

Combine cream cheese, butter, sugars, & egg, mixing well. Combine dry ingredients; add oil, milk & 2 eggs, mixing well. Fold in nuts. Spread 1 cup of batter into greased loaf pan. Top with cream cheese mixture; cover with remaining batter. Bake at 350⁰ for 1 hour.

Microwave Bread Pudding
Vicki Richburg, Six Mile, SC

2 1/2 c. milk
2 c. dry bread cubes
2 Tbs. cornstarch
1/2 c. raisins
1/3 c. sugar

1/2 tsp. cinnamon
1/2 tsp. vanilla
1/4 tsp. salt
3 egg yolks, beaten

Microwave milk in a 4 c. measuring bowl, on high 4 to 6 minutes. In a 2 qt. casserole, toss bread, cornstarch, raisins, sugar, cinnamon, vanilla and salt. Gradually stir in milk, then eggs. Microwave on high 2 minutes, stirring occasionally. Reduce power 50 %, 4 to 8 minutes or until almost set in center, gently pushing outer edges toward center every 3 minutes. *Do Not Over Cook.* Let stand on countertop at least 30 minutes.

Banana Nut Bread
Jennifer Fellure, Milton, FL

2 1/2 c. self-rising flour
1 c. sugar
3 Tbs. salad oil
3/4 c. milk

1 egg
1 c. mashed bananas
1 c. chopped pecans

Mix all ingredients together and pour into 2 small greased loaf pans. Bake in 350⁰ oven for approximately 1 hour.

Monkey Bread
Mary Jackson, Lexington, NC

3 cans biscuits
1 1/2 c. confectioners sugar
1/2 c. brown sugar

1/2 to 3/4 c. chopped pecans
2 Tbs. cinnamon
1 stick margarine, melted

Mix sugars, cinnamon and nuts. Dip biscuits in butter, roll in mixture, stand biscuits up in a bundt pan. Bake at 350⁰ for 45 minutes.

Wheat Waffles
Selected

1 egg, separated	1 Tbs. sugar
3/4 c. milk	1 to 2 tsp. grated orange peel
1/3 c. oil	1 tsp. baking powder
1/4 c. orange juice	1/4 tsp. salt
1 c. whole wheat flour	

In small mixing bowl, beat the egg white until stiff; set aside. In another mixing bowl, beat egg yolk, milk, oil and orange juice. Combine flour, sugar, orange peel, baking powder and salt. Stir into milk mixture. Fold in egg white. Bake in preheated waffle iron until golden brown.

Waffle Mix
Madeline Darnell, Sulphur, LA

1 1/2 c. self rising flour	1 egg
1/2 c. uncooked oatmeal	1 c. milk
1/2 tsp. cinnamon	

Preheat waffle iron. Mix flour, oatmeal and cinnamon in mixing bowl. Add egg and slowly add milk until all gone. Oil waffle iron lightly and pour batter into iron. Bake until golden brown. Yields 4.

Cinnamon-Pecan Rolls
Selected

1/3 c. chopped pecans	1 8 oz. pkg. crescent rolls
1/4 tsp. cinnamon	2 Tbs. melted butter or butter flavored
1/3 c. packed brown sugar	cooking spray

Combine pecans, brown sugar and cinnamon; set aside. Separate rolls at perforation point and spray one side with cooking spray or brush with butter. Sprinkle with sugar mixture and roll according to package directions. Place on lightly greased baking sheet. Bake 10 - 12 minutes at 400⁰.

Sweet Potato Biscuits
Selected

1 c. cooked, mashed
  sweet potatoes
1/3 c. margarine, melted
1 egg, beaten

1 c. sifted flour
2 tsp. baking powder
1/2 tsp. salt

Combine potatoes, margarine and egg in bowl. Sift flour, baking powder and salt together; blend into potato mixture. Roll, cut, and bake at 350^0 until brown.

Gingerbread Men
Selected

1/2 c. molasses
1/4 c. sugar
3 Tbs. butter
1 Tbs. milk
2 c. flour
1/2 tsp. baking soda

1/2 tsp. salt
1/2 tsp. nutmeg
1/2 tsp. cinnamon
1/2 tsp. powdered cloves
1/2 tsp. ginger

Heat molasses to the boiling point. Add sugar, butter and milk. Sift together remaining ingredients and add to the first mixture. Add more flour if necessary to make dough thick enough to roll out. Cut as desired. Bake about 8 minutes at 375^0.

Crunchy Banana Muffins
Madeline Darnell, Sulphur, LA

1 c. oatmeal
1 c. whole wheat flour
1/4 tsp. salt
1/2 c. skim milk
2 bananas, mashed

1/3 c. honey
2 1/2 tsp. baking powder
1/4 tsp. baking soda
1 egg

Mix all ingredients. Put in muffin pan. Bake at 350^0 for 15 - 18 minutes. Makes 8.

26

Cinnamon Rolls

Kim Patterson, Emporia, VA

2 c. all purpose flour
1 pkg. active dry yeast
1 c. milk
1/3 c. sugar
1/3 c. butter

1 tsp. salt
2 eggs
3 Tbs. butter,
1/2 c. sugar and
   2 Tbs. cinnamon to coat buns

In a mixer bowl combine flour and yeast. Heat milk, 1/3 c. sugar, butter and salt just until warm, stirring constantly. Add to flour mixture; add eggs. Beat at low speed for 1/2 minute. Beat 3 minutes at high speed. Stir in as much flour as you can mix with a spoon. On a floured surface knead in enough remaining flour to make a moderately stiff dough that is smooth and elastic, 6 to 8 minutes total. Shape into a ball in a greased bowl; turn once. Cover, let rise in a warm place till double in size, about 1 hour. Punch down, divide in half. Cover, let rise 10 minutes. Roll 1/2 of dough in 12 x 8 rectangle. Melt 3 Tbs. butter; spread half over dough. Combine 1/2 c. sugar and 2 Tbs. cinnamon; sprinkle half over dough. Roll up jelly roll style beginning from longest side. Seal. Slice into 12 pieces for small rolls or 6 for large. Place in greased round baking pans. Repeat with remaining dough. Cover, let rise until doubled in size, about 30 minutes. Bake at 375⁰ for 20 to 25 minutes.

Icing:
Combine: 1 c. powdered sugar, 1/4 tsp. vanilla and enough milk for drizzling. Drizzle on rolls when they cool.

Multi-Grain Baking Mix

Selected

6 c. all-purpose flour
2 c. whole wheat flour
1 c. quick-cooking rolled oats

5 Tbs. baking powder
1 Tbs. salt
1 1/2 c. shortening

In a very large bowl, combine all ingredients, except shortening. Using pastry blender or fork, cut in shortening until crumbly. Transfer to lightly covered container. Use as directed in muffins, breads, etc. May keep refrigerated for up to 4 weeks. Yields 12 cups.

Amish Friendship Bread

Selected

(Use wooden spoon)
Starter:
1 c. sugar   1 c. milk
1 c. flour

Stir with wooden spoon, once a day for 10 days. Divide into 3 individual cups. Put 2 cups away; keep 1 cup and follow recipe starting with Day 1.

Day 1 - Do nothing
Days 2,3,4 - Stir with wooden spoon.
Day 5 - Add 1 c. milk, 1 c. flour, 1 c. sugar. Stir with wooden spoon.
Days 6,7,8,9 - Stir with wooden spoon
Day 10 - Add 1 c. milk, 1 c. flour, 1 c. sugar. Stir with wooden spoon.
Pour into 3 containers of 1 c. each . Give to friends with recipe and keep 1 cup for your starter.

Add to remaining batch on 10th day:
1 c. oil   1 c. chopped nuts
1 c. sugar   1 tsp. vanilla
2 c. flour   3 eggs
1/2 c. milk   1 tsp. cinnamon
1/2 tsp. baking powder   1/2 tsp. salt
1/2 tsp. soda   1 large box instant vanilla pudding

Pour into 2 greased and floured loaf pans. Bake at 350^0 for 40 - 50 minutes. Cool 10 minutes and remove from pans.

America has more to eat than any country in the world and more diets to keep us from eating it.

She riseth also while it is yet night, and giveth meat to her household, and a portion to her maidens. Proverbs 31:15

Fold in whipped topping. Pour into crust and sprinkle with coconut. Chill.
Opt. - Use toasted coconut.

Carrot & Raisin Salad

Selected

16 oz. bag of carrots
1/2 c. raisins
2 Tbs. mayonnaise

1 c. miniature marshmallows
1/2 c. crushed pineapple, drained

Wash and peel carrots. Grate carrots into bowl. Add all other ingredients and
mix. Cover and chill for one hour.

29

Sugar-Free Cherry Coke Salad
Selected

1 can cherries
1 1/2 c. water
2 sm. boxes cherry sugar-free
  Jell-O

10 pkgs. Equal
1 can crushed pineapple in juice
8 oz. diet Coke
1/2 c. chopped nuts

Bring cherries and water to a boil; remove from heat. Add Jell-O and stir well to dissolve. When mixture cools add Equal, pineapple, Coke and nuts. Chill for one hour.

Shrimp Salad
Selected

3 c. lettuce, shredded
2 c. cucumbers, chopped
2 c. cooked corkscrew macaroni
1/4 c. fresh parsley, chopped
1 1/2 c. celery, sliced

2 c. tomatoes, chopped
1 lb. cooked, small shrimp
8 oz. bottle bacon & tomato salad
  dressing
1/2 c. sour cream

Layer lettuce, cucumber, macaroni, parsley, celery, tomatoes, shrimp in a large salad bowl. Combine salad dressing and sour cream. Spread over top of salad. Cover and chill. Toss before serving.

Vegetable Salad
Selected

Drain and mix together:

1 can each of shoe peg corn, young peas, French style green beans
2 oz. jar pimentos   1/2 c. celery, chopped

Boil to dissolve sugar, then cool. Pour over vegetables and refrigerate.

1/2 c. oil
1/2 c. vinegar

1/2 c. sugar

Fruit Salad

Amanda Doyle, Groveton, TX

1 can pie filling (peach, cherry)
2 pkg. frozen strawberries
1 can chunk pineapple (drained)

1 can mandarin oranges, drained
2 bananas, sliced

Mix and refrigerate overnight.

Garden Bean Salad

Selected

1 16 oz. can cut green beans
2 16 oz. cans lima beans
1 16 oz. can kidney beans
1 16 oz. can wax beans
1 16 oz. can garbanzo beans
1 lg. green pepper, chopped
3 celery stalks, chopped

1 12 oz. jar sliced pimento, drained
1 bunch green onions, sliced
2 c. vinegar
2 c. sugar
1/2 c. water
1 tsp. salt

Drain all cans of beans; place in a large bowl. Add green pepper, celery, pimiento and green onions; set aside. Bring remaining ingredients to a boil in a heavy saucepan; boil for 5 minutes. Remove from heat and immediately pour over vegetables. Refrigerate several hours.

Fancy Fruit Salad

Jennifer Fellure, Milton, FL

1 lg. can sliced peaches, drained
1 small can pineapple tidbits,
   do not drain
2 pkgs. frozen strawberries,
   thawed in refrigerator

3 bananas sliced
1- 3 oz. pkg. vanilla instant pudding
2 Tbs. Tang, instant orange drink

Place fruit in large bowl in order given. Mix together the dry pudding and dry Tang. Sprinkle over fruit and gently mix. Let stand several hours in refrigerator before serving.

Cranberry Salad

Maddy Ray, Phoenix, AZ

1 lb. fresh cranberries
2 - 3 oz. pkg. cherry Jell-O
2 c. sugar
2 c. hot water

1 1/2 c. cranberry juice
1 can crushed pineapple, drained
3 or 4 apples (peeled & chopped)

Chop cranberries very fine in food processor; mix with sugar. Dissolve Jell-O in hot water, adding cranberry juice, crushed pineapple (drained), and chopped apples. Mix well and refrigerate. Nuts or mandarin oranges, optional.

Cranberry Salad

Madeline Darnell, Sulphur, LA

12 oz. bag cranberries
1/2 c. sugar
1 - 3 oz. orange Jell-O
1 1/2 c. boiling water
1 c. cold water

1 Tbs. lemon juice
1/4 tsp. cinnamon
1/8 tsp. cloves
1 orange, diced
1/2 c. walnuts, almonds, or celery

Chop cranberries very fine in a food processor; mix with sugar and set aside. Dissolve Jell-O in boiling water; add cold water, lemon juice, cinnamon, and cloves. Refrigerate until thick. Fold in cranberries, orange and nuts. Spoon into 5 cup mold that has been sprayed with Pam. Refrigerate until firm.

Pasta Salad

Norma Moore, Tyro, NC

16 oz. cooked curly pasta,
    drained and cooled
4 boiled eggs, diced
1 lg. onion, chopped
1 sweet pepper, chopped

1 can light Treet, diced
1 16 oz. can tomatoes
1 16 oz. can green peas
Light salt to the pasta
1 c. mayonnaise

Mix all together with 1 c. mayonnaise. If dry, add more mayonnaise. Note: Carrots or other vegetables can be added.

Sea Foam Salad
Maddy Ray, Tempe, AZ

2 - 8 oz. pkg. cream cheese,
  softened
2 small tubs Cool Whip
2 sm. cans crushed pineapple,
  (in juice)

1 - 3 oz. instant pistachio pudding
1/2 c. chopped pecans
1 c. miniature marshmallows
Add 2 drops green coloring

Mix all ingredients and chill.

Watergate Salad
Mary Fellure, Milton, FL

1 lg. can crushed pineapple
1 box pistachio pudding
1 - 8 oz. Cool Whip

1 c. miniature marshmallows
1 c. chopped nuts

Mix pineapple and pudding thoroughly. Add Cool Whip and mix. Fold in marshmallows and nuts. Mix and chill. Note: Coconut can be added.

Heavenly Hash
Norma Moore, Tyro, NC

1 sm. can pineapple chunks,
  drained
1 can coconut
1 small pkg. miniature
  marshmallows

8 oz. can fruit cocktail, drained
1/2 c. chopped pecans
1/2 c. maraschino cherries
1 lg. Cool Whip

Mix all ingredients and refrigerate overnight.

Taco Salad

Pat Mangus, Louisville, KY

1 lb. ground beef	Nacho chips
1 pkg. taco seasoning	Salsa or favorite salad dressing
3/4 c. water	

Lettuce, tomato, peppers, olives, green onions; whatever you like. Cook and drain meat. Add taco seasoning and water. Simmer for 20 minutes. When meat has cooled, mix with lettuce mixture. Crush nacho chips and add last. Use favorite dressing or salsa.

Macaroni Salad

Letha Ray, Salt Rock, WV

2 c. macaroni, cooked, drained & cooled	2 Tbs. onion chopped
	1 to 1/2 c. mayonnaise
1/2 c. celery chopped	1 to 1/2 c. mayonnaise
1/2 c. green pepper chopped	Salt & pepper to taste

In a large bowl stir in mayonnaise, vinegar, and salt & pepper until well blended; add macaroni, celery, green peppers, and onion. Toss to coat well. Cover and refrigerate at least 2 hours.

Hot Macaroni Salad

Selected

1 can cream of mushroom soup	2 c. cooked macaroni, drained
1/2 c. milk	1 chopped onion
1/2 c. mayonnaise	1/4 c. pimentos, chopped
1 green pepper, chopped	1 1/2 c. grated longhorn cheese

In a small saucepan combine soup, milk and mayonnaise. Place over low heat and stir until well mixed. Add the remaining ingredients. Top with cheese. Bake at 350^0 until heated thoroughly, about 30 minutes.

Chicken Salad

Faye Chapman, Milton, WV

4 halved chicken breasts	3/4 c. plain yogurt
1/3 c. chopped celery	3/4 c. mayonaise
1 18 oz. can crushed pineapple	Salt & pepper to taste
1/4 c. chopped nuts	

Boil chicken and season as you like. Cut up chicken into small pieces and add celery, pineapple, and nuts. Mix mayonnaise and yogurt together. Mix adding a little at a time so you don't get too much. Better if refrigerated overnight.

Frozen Strawberry Salad

Donna Lisenbee, Boaz, AL

1 c. Eagle Brand milk	2 c. strawberries, chopped
1/4 c. lemon juice	8 oz. whipped topping
8 oz. crushed pineapple	

Combine all ingredients and freeze until set.

Strawberry Fluff

Nancy Schrader, San Antonio, TX

28 oz. small curd cottage cheese	1 small can crushed pineapple, drained
2 small boxes strawberry Jell-O	1 lg. Cool Whip
1 mashed banana	

Mix dry Jell-O with cottage cheese. Add pineapple and banana. Fold in Cool Whip. Refrigerate.

Strawberry Glazed Fruit Salad

Selected

1 qt. fresh strawberries, halved	4 firm bananas, sliced
1 c. pineapple chunks, drained	16 oz. strawberry glaze

In large mixing bowl, mix the three ingredients and fold in glaze. Chill.

Fruit Salad

Chris Perrine, Milton, FL

2 cans fruit cocktail, drained
1 c. chopped pecans
2 sm. cans pineapple tidbits
Lg. box strawberry Jell-O

1 small box instant vanilla pudding
2 bananas, sliced
2 apples, chopped

Mix all ingredients and chill.

Red Cabbage Salad

Mary Fellure, Milton, FL

4 c. coarsely chopped red cabbage
3 green onions, chopped
1/4 c. fresh parsley, chopped

1 medium tomato, coarsely chopped
1 small cucumber, peeled and chopped
Salt & pepper to taste

Combine ingredients and dress with your favorite dressing.

Pistachio Salad

Kate Cravatt, Brewton, AL

1 (12 oz.) Cool Whip
1 can coconut
1 lg. can crushed pineapple

1 small pkg. pistachio instant pudding
1 c. chopped pecans
1 c. miniature marshmallows

Mix ingredients together and chill. Keep refrigerated.

Lime Jell-O Salad

Geraldine Chapman, Brunswick, GA

1 small pkg. lime Jell-O
1 c. boiling water
1 small pkg. cream cheese
1/4 c. mayonnaise

1/4 c. cream
1 small can crushed pineapple
1 c. chopped nuts

Mix Jell-O with boiling water. Mix cream cheese, mayonnaise, cream, pineapple and nuts. Add to Jell-O. Refrigerate until congealed.

Cole Slaw

Ann Shaw, Groveton, TX

1 head of cabbage, chopped	1/4 c. milk
16 oz. salad dressing	Salt & pepper to taste
1/8 c. of vinegar	1 grated carrot

Mix above ingredients and chill at least 1 hour. Makes 8 servings.

Cauliflower Salad

Ann Pritchard, Cleveland, Ohio

1 head lettuce	1 pkg. dry Good Seasons Italian
1 head cauliflower	Dressing
1 16 oz. pkg. frozen peas	1/2 c. crisp, crumbled bacon
2 c. real mayonaise	1/2 c. Parmesan cheese

Tear lettuce and cauliflower into bite size pieces in large container. Add defrosted, raw peas. Spread all exposed vegetables with mayonnaise. Sprinkle with Italian dressing, bacon, and Parmesan cheese. Cover tightly and refrigerate 24 hours or more.

Broccoli Salad

Ann Pritchard, Cleveland, Ohio

2 bunches of raw broccoli, cut into pieces	1 medium onion, chopped
	1 lb. bacon, cooked & crumbled

Dressing:

1 c. mayonnaise	2 tsp. sugar
2 Tbs. vinegar	

Combine broccoli, onion & bacon. Mix dressing and pour over broccoli mixture. Marinate 1 to 2 hours.

Three Day Slaw

Betty Thomas, Greenville, NC

1 medium cabbage head, chopped fine
2 medium onions, sliced in thin rings
1 c. sugar, sprinkled on cut-up cabbage & onions

Bring to boil:
1 c. vinegar   1 tsp. celery seed
3/4 c. salad oil   1 tsp. salt
1 tsp. dry mustard

Sprinkle sugar over cut-up cabbage and onions. Boil mixture and pour over cabbage mixture slowly. Let mixture stay in refrigerator for three days.

Apricot-Delight Salad

Betty Thomas, Greenville, NC

2 small boxes apricot Jell-O   2 bananas, sliced
2 c. hot water   2 c. miniature marshmallows
2 c. cold water
1 #2 can drained crushed pineapple (save juice)

Mix first three ingredients and let congeal slightly. Add pineapple, bananas and marshmallows. Chill until firm.

Topping:
1/2 c. pineapple juice   1 8 oz. pkg. cream cheese
3/4 c. sugar   1 pkg. Dream Whip
1 egg   1 can flaked coconut
2 Tbs. flour

Cook pineapple juice, sugar, egg and flour until thick. Add cream cheese; stir until smooth. Let cool. Mix Dream Whip as directed on box; fold in. Spread over Jell-O; sprinkle coconut on top and chill.

Mustard Potato Salad
Selected

2 c. diced, peeled potatoes (1 lb.)
2 eggs, well boiled
1/4 c. mayonnaise

1 tsp. prepared mustard
1/2 tsp. dried minced onion
1/4 tsp. salt

In a saucepan, cover potatoes with water and cook until tender. Drain and cool. In a bowl, combine eggs, mayonnaise, mustard, onion and salt. Stir in cooled potatoes. Cover and chill.

Classic Macaroni Salad
Selected

7 oz. elbow macaroni,
  cooked & drained
2 eggs, hard boiled

1/2 c. chopped green pepper
1/2 c. mayonnaise
2 oz. jar chopped pimientos

In a bowl, combine eggs, macaroni, green pepper, mayonnaise and pimientos. Cover and chill.

Ambrosia Waldorf Salad
Selected

2 c. fresh or frozen cranberries,
  chopped
1/2 c. sugar
3 c. miniature marshmallows
2 c. diced, unpeeled apples
1 c. seedless green grapes, halved

3/4 c. chopped pecans
1 - 20 oz. can pineapple tidbits,
  drained
1 c. heavy cream, whipped
Flaked coconut

Combine cranberries and sugar. In a large bowl, combine the marshmallows, apples, grapes, pecans and pineapple. Add cranberries and mix well. Fold in whipped cream. Cover and chill. Sprinkle coconut on last.

Ambrosia Fruit Salad
Selected

20 oz. pineapple tidbits
1/4 c. brown sugar
1/2 tsp. grated orange peel

2 medium oranges, peeled and cut
2 medium apples, peeled and diced
1 Tbs. flaked coconut

Drain pineapple, reserving 1/4 c. juice in a saucepan; set pineapple aside. Add brown sugar and orange peel to the juice; heat until sugar dissolves. Peel and section oranges into a large bowl, reserving juice; add the apples and pineapples. Add pineapple juice mixture and stir. Chill. Sprinkle with coconut just before serving.

A new Chinese diet: eat all you can, but use only one chopstick.

Nevertheless he left not himself without witness, in that he did good, and gave us rain from heaven, and fruitful seasons, filling our hearts with food and gladness. Acts 14:17

Broccoli Casserole
Selected

1 c. water	1/4 c. chopped celery
1/2 tsp. salt	1 can cream of mushroom soup
1 c. instant rice	1 can cream of celery soup
1/4 c. margarine	1 pkg. frozen chopped broccoli, thawed
1/4 c. chopped onions	1/2 c. diced American cheese

Bring water and salt to boil. Add rice, cover, and remove from heat to let stand for 5 minutes. Melt butter in skillet; sauté onions and celery until tender. In large mixing bowl, combine rice, celery, and onions with remaining ingredients. Pour into a greased casserole dish and bake at 350^0 for one hour.

Green Bean Casserole
Norma Moore, Tyro, NC

2 cans French style green beans, drained well	8 oz. sour cream
8 oz. cheddar cheese, grated	Bread crumbs

Mix all ingredients, except bread crumbs. Cover top with bread crumbs. Bake uncovered 1 hour at 350^0. Sprinkle some cheese on top of crumbs (optional).

Country Green Beans
Selected

1 lb. fresh green beans, trimmed & cut	1/4 c. butter
1/4 c. onion, chopped	1 garlic clove, minced
1/4 c. cooked ham	1 1/4 c. water
	Salt & pepper to taste

In a saucepan combine all ingredients. Cover and simmer 50 minutes or until beans are tender.

Tangy Tomato Slices
Selected

1 c. vegetable oil	1/2 tsp. pepper
1/3 c. vinegar	1/2 tsp. dried mustard
1/4 c. minced fresh parsley	1/2 tsp. garlic powder
1 Tbs. dried basil	1 medium sweet onion, thinly sliced
1 Tbs. sugar	6 lg. tomatoes, sliced
1 tsp. salt	

In a small bowl, mix the first nine ingredients. Layer onions and tomatoes in a shallow dish. Pour the marinated mixture over; cover and refrigerate for several hours.

Pineapple Beets
Selected

2 Tbs. brown sugar	1 can sliced beets, drained
1 Tbs. cornstarch	1 Tbs. butter
1/4 tsp. salt	1 Tbs. lemon juice
8 oz. can pineapple tidbits, undrained	

In a saucepan, combine brown sugar, cornstarch and salt; add pineapple and bring to a boil, stirring constantly until thick. Add the beets, butter and lemon juice; cook over medium heat for five minutes, stirring occasionally. Yields 4 servings.

Beets
Selected

1 lb. can diced beets, drained reserving 1/3 c. liquid	1/4 tsp. salt
2 Tbs. sugar	1/4. c. vinegar
1 Tbs. cornstarch	2 Tbs. margarine

In saucepan, combine sugar, cornstarch, salt, 1/3 c. reserved liquid, vinegar and margarine. Cook and stir until mixture thickens. Add beets and heat thoroughly.

Quick Baked Beans

Selected

3 to 4 strips of bacon
1 clove of garlic, minced
1 onion, chopped
1/2 green pepper, chopped

1/2 pound ground beef
Salt & pepper to taste
1 lb. can pork & beans
2 hot dogs, sliced

Cook the bacon until crisp. Set aside. Sauté garlic, onion and green pepper in bacon drippings until brown. Add beef; brown well and drain. Season with salt and pepper. Stir in beans and hot dogs. Cover and simmer on low heat for 10 minutes. Crumble bacon and put on top.

Baked Beans

Selected

1 lb. ground beef
1/2 c. finely chopped onions
1/2 tsp. salt
1/4 tsp. pepper
1/4 tsp. Tabasco sauce

2 Tbs. vinegar
2 Tbs. brown sugar
1 16 oz. can pork & beans
1/2 c. catsup

Cook ground beef and onion in small amount of fat in a heavy skillet. Drain, add remaining ingredients, and mix well. Put in casserole dish and bake at 350⁰ for 30 minutes.

Cheese Potatoes

Mary Fellure, Milton, FL

6 lg. potatoes
1 tsp. salt
3/4 c. margarine

8 oz. cheddar cheese, shredded
1 c. milk
2 eggs, beaten

Wash and cut potatoes; place in large pot and cover with water and 1/2 tsp. salt. Cook potatoes until tender and drain. Mash potatoes until very smooth. In saucepan, cook and stir butter, cheese, milk and remaining salt until smooth. Stir in potatoes and eggs. Pour into greased baking dish and bake uncovered for 40 minutes at 350⁰ until puffy and golden brown.

Baked Potato Spears

Donna Lisenbee, Boaz, AL

3 lg. potatoes, cut into long wedges
1/4 c. Miracle Whip salad dressing
Onion salt & pepper to taste

Brush potatoes with dressing. Season with salt and pepper. Place on greased baking sheet and bake at 375⁰ for 50 minutes or until tender and brown.

Scalloped Potatoes

Selected

8 to 10 medium potatoes
  (sliced thin)
1 onion, sliced &
  separated into onion rings
1 c. grated cheese

1/8 Tbs. flour
2 tsp. pepper
2 tsp. salt
1 lg. can evaporated milk

Alternate layers of potatoes, onions, cheese and flour. Season lightly with salt and pepper. Pour milk over potatoes. Cover and bake at 350⁰ for 1 hour. Take cover off and continue to bake 30 more minutes.

Paprika Potatoes

Selected

4 lg. potatoes, peeled, quartered & cooked
3 Tbs. butter
1/2 tsp. paprika

In a large skillet, slowly sauté potatoes in butter until golden brown, about 15 minutes. Sprinkle with paprika.

Baked Parmesan Potatoes

Mary Jackson, Lexington, NC

6 medium potatoes,
  peeled and quartered
1/4 c. flour
1/4 c. Parmesan cheese

3/4 tsp. salt
1/4 tsp. pepper
6 Tbs. margarine

Combine flour, cheese, salt and pepper in bag. Moisten potatoes and shake in flour mixture, coating well. Melt margarine in shallow baking pan and place potatoes in one layer in pan. Bake in 425^0 oven for one hour, turning once during baking.

Potato Casserole

Jennifer Fellure, Milton, FL

2 lb. pkg. frozen hash browns
1 can cream of chicken soup
3/4 c. chopped onions
1 16 oz. sour cream

2 c. grated cheddar cheese
Salt & pepper to taste
1 c. bread crumbs
Melted margarine

Mix together the first six ingredients and put in 13 x 9 pan. Combine 1 cup or more of bread crumbs with melted margarine. Spread evenly over potato mixture and bake at 350^0 for 1 hour.

New Red Potatoes

Selected

2 Tbs. margarine
2 to 3 lb. new red potatoes, cubed
1 1/2 c. sliced carrots
3/4 c. chopped onion

1/4 c. fresh parsley, minced
1 garlic clove, minced
1/4 tsp. salt
1/4 tsp. pepper

In large skillet melt butter, add potatoes & carrots, and toss to coat. Add remaining ingredients and cook over medium heat for 20 minutes or until vegetables are tender.

Marinated Carrots
Letha Ray, Salt Rock, WV

Lg. bag carrots, sliced & cooked
1 green pepper, sliced in rings
1 med. Vidalia onion, sliced
1 can tomato soup
1 c. sugar
1 tsp. salt

3/4 c. vinegar
1/2 c. salad oil
1 tsp. mustard
2 tsp. Worcestershire sauce
1/2 tsp. pepper

Place cooked carrots, green peppers and onions in large bowl. Mix remaining ingredients and pour over carrot mixture. Refrigerate for several hours.

Broccoli Casserole
Chris Perrine, Milton, FL

1 c. rice, uncooked
1 c. water
1/3 c. chopped onion
1/2 stick margarine

1 pkg. frozen broccoli, thawed
1/2 c. mushroom soup
1 - 8 oz. Cheese Whiz

Mix all ingredients and bake at 350⁰ for one hour.

Broccoli Rolls
Maddy Ray, Tempe, AZ

1 - 10 oz., cut broccoli, cooked
  & drained
2/3 c. melted margarine
1 lg. onion, chopped fine
1/2 tsp. red pepper

6 eggs, beaten
1/2 c. Parmesan cheese
1/2 tsp. garlic salt
1 tsp. black pepper
3 c. Pepperidge Farm stuffing mix

Mix all ingredients in large bowl; chill for one hour. Roll into small balls. Bake at 325⁰ for 15 to 25 minutes on a greased cookie sheet.

Squash Casserole
Julie Waller, New Caney, TX

4 or 5 summer squash
1 stick butter
1 small onion, chopped
1/2 c. bell pepper, chopped
1/2 c. chopped celery
1 box Stove Top dressing (chicken flavor)

1 can cream of chicken soup
2 eggs (beaten)
Black pepper, salt & sage to taste
1 c. milk
Grated cheese

Cook squash. Melt butter and sauté with onion, green pepper, and celery. Add soup, eggs, pepper, salt and sage. Cook dressing; add milk. Mix all together; top with grated cheese. Bake at 350⁰ for 30 minutes.

Squash Casserole
Joyce Winstead, Wilson, NC

6 c. sliced summer squash
1/4 c. chopped onions
1 can cream of chicken soup
1 c. sour cream

1 c. shredded carrots
1 pkg. corn bread stuffing mix
1/2 c. margarine

Cook squash and onions in boiling water for five minutes. Drain. Combine soup and sour cream; stir in carrots. Fold in drained squash. Combine stuffing mix and margarine; spread half of the stuffing mix in bottom of baking dish, 9 x 11 x 2. Spoon vegetable mixture on top. Sprinkle remaining stuffing mixture over vegetables. Bake at 350⁰ for 25 to 30 minutes.

Easy Tater-Tot Casserole
Selected

1 lb. ground beef
  (cooked & drained)
1 - 2 lb. pkg. tater-tot potatoes

1 onion, diced
Salt & pepper to taste
1 can cream of mushroom soup

Crumble ground beef and place in casserole dish. Cover with onion, salt and pepper. Pour soup over all and top with tater-tots. Bake at 350⁰ for 30-40 minutes.

Skillet Hash Brown Meal

Maddy Ray, Tempe, AZ

6 slices bacon
6 eggs, beaten
1/4 c. milk
1 12 oz. pkg. frozen hash brown potatoes
  (with onion, red & green pepper)

Salt & pepper to taste
1 c. shredded cheddar cheese

Cook bacon, remove and drain part of drippings; add potatoes, cook over low heat. Combine eggs, milk, salt & pepper. Stir well and pour over potatoes. Top with cheese and sprinkle with bacon. Cover and cook over low heat 10 minutes.

Eggplant Casserole

Lamar McCabe, Waycross, GA

1 eggplant, chopped
2 eggs
Milk (about 1/4 c.)

Saltine crackers (about 1/2 pkg.)
8 oz. mild cheddar cheese

Cook eggplant until tender. Drain. Add eggs, milk, saltines and cheese, grated. Bake at 350° for 25 to 30 minutes until bubbly. Reserve some cheese for topping.

Sweet Potato Crunch

Mary Fellure, Milton, FL

#2 can sweet potatoes, mashed
1/8 tsp. salt
2 eggs
1/3 c. evaporated milk

1 stick margarine, melted
3/4 c. sugar
1 tsp. vanilla

Mix well the above ingredients, pour into casserole dish, and top with the following mixture.

1 c. light brown sugar
1/2 c. self-rising flour
1/2 tsp. baking powder

1/3 c. margarine, melted
1 c. chopped pecans

Top casserole and bake at 350° for 30 minutes.

48

Broccoli Casserole
Susan Taylor, Brunswick, GA

2 pkgs. cooked broccoli
2 eggs
1 c. mayonnaise
1 medium onion, grated

1 c. cheese, grated
1 c. cream of mushroom soup
·Salt & pepper to taste
1 c. cracker crumbs

Mix above ingredients together except crumbs. Top with cracker crumbs. Bake at 350⁰ for about 30 minutes.

Sweet Potato Casserole
Lanee Osborn, New Caney, TX

3 c. cooked, mashed sweet
  potatoes
2 eggs (beaten)
1/2 c. milk
1 stick butter, softened

1 sm. can crushed pineapple
1 c. sugar
1/4 tsp. salt
1 tsp. vanilla

Mix all ingredients well. Place in casserole dish that has been sprayed with Pam.

Topping:
1 c. brown sugar
1 c. pecans, chopped

1 stick butter

Mix well; spoon over mixture. Bake at 350⁰ 30 min. or until brown.

Candied Yams
Norma Moore, Tyro, NC

1 lg. can sweet potatoes (29 oz.)
1/2 c. sugar
3 Tbs. plain flour, optional
1/2 tsp. nutmeg

1/2 tsp. cinnamon
1/2 stick margarine
1 tsp. vanilla

Drain potatoes; layer across dish. Sprinkle sugar, flour, cinnamon, nutmeg, and vanilla over potatoes. Dot with butter. Place another layer of potatoes; continue to top of dish. Bake at 350⁰ 30 min. or until brown.

Baked Squash

Gladys Coker, New Caney, TX

5 lbs. squash	1/4 c. sugar
2 eggs	2 Tbs. cooked onion (sauté)
1 c. bread crumbs	Salt & pepper to taste
1 stick butter	Additional bread crumbs

Cook squash until tender. Drain and mash. Add all ingredients. Put in greased casserole dish; cover with more bread crumbs. Bake 350° until brown.

Yellow Squash Casserole

Selected

2 c. cooked yellow squash	1 tsp. salt
1 can cream of chicken soup	1/2 tsp. pepper
1 c. sour cream	Herb seasoned bread crumbs
1 carrot, grated	1 Tbs. butter
1 small onion, chopped	1/4 c. grated cheddar cheese

Mash squash in a bowl; add soup, sour cream, carrot, onion, salt & pepper. Spray casserole dish with non-stick spray. Cover casserole dish with bread crumbs. Add squash mixture. Cover with additional bread crumbs and dot with butter. Bake at 350° for 35 minutes. Remove from oven and sprinkle with cheese. Let stand 10 to 15 minutes before serving.

Southern Corn Pudding

Mary Fellure, Milton, FL

6 ears fresh corn	1/4 to 1/2 tsp. black pepper
1 1/4 Tbs. flour	1/2 c. milk
2 Tbs. melted margarine	2 eggs
1/2 tsp. salt	

Preheat oven to 375° and grease an 8 inch casserole dish with non-stick vegetable shortening. Stand each ear on end and cut off kernels with a sharp knife. Then scrape the cobs to get the juice and pulp. Mix corn and pulp with remaining ingredients and blend well. Pour into casserole dish and bake 30 - 40 minutes or until firm and a knife inserted in the middle comes out clean.

Augratin Potatoes

Selected

4 oz. sharp cheddar cheese
2/3 lb. Velveeta cheese
2 sticks margarine

1 pt. half & half
2 lb. bag frozen hash browns

Melt both cheeses, butter and milk. Pour over potatoes in 9 x 13 pan. Bake at 350⁰ for 1 hour.

Mushroom Scalloped Potatoes

Iva Gilkerson, Huntington, WV

4 or 5 med. potatoes, sliced thin
1 small onion, sliced thin

Salt & pepper to taste
1 can cream of mushroom soup

Peel and slice potatoes and onions very thin. Salt & pepper them to your taste. Pour mushroom soup mixed with 1 can of water over the potatoes, enough to cover them. Bake in 350⁰ oven for approximately 1 hour or until potatoes are tender.

Vegetable Medley

Selected

16 oz. each: frozen broccoli, carrots, & cauliflower, thawed & drained
1 can cream of chicken soup   1/4 tsp. black pepper
1 c. cheddar cheese, shredded   1 can french fried onions
1/3 c. sour cream

Combine vegetables, soup, 1/2 c. cheese, sour cream, pepper and 1/2 can French fried onions. Pour into covered casserole dish and bake at 350⁰ for 30 minutes. Top with remaining cheese and onions. Bake uncovered 5 minutes longer.

Zucchini Bake

Selected

4 eggs, beaten
1/2 c. oil
2 c. zucchini, raw, thinly sliced
1 medium onion, chopped

1 c. Bisquick mix
1/2 c. Parmesan cheese
1/2 tsp. each: parsley, salt,
   garlic salt, & basil

Mix and stir all ingredients together. Bake in greased baking dish at 350⁰ for 30 to 40 minutes or until lightly browned.

Glazed Baby Carrots

Selected

3 c. baby carrots
1/2 c. leeks, sliced
2 Tbs. water
6 oz. can unsweetened
   pineapple juice

2 Tbs. cornstarch
1/2 tsp. grated ginger root
1/8 tsp. ground nutmeg
1/2 tsp. salt

Wash and trim carrots. Combine carrots, leeks and water. In microwave safe casserole dish, cover and microwave for 8 to 10 minutes or until crisp tender. Stir once or twice and drain. Combine juice, cornstarch, ginger root, and salt. Cook uncovered on high for 2 1/2 to 3 minutes or until thickened, stirring every minute. Pour the glaze over carrots; stir to coat.

Glazed Carrots

Selected

1 bunch carrots, peeled
   and cooked
3 Tbs. butter

1/2 c. honey
2 Tbs. orange juice

Combine all ingredients in a skillet and cook until liquid is reduced and carrots are glazed thoroughly.

Spiced Carrot Strips
Selected

5 or 6 lg. carrots, julienned	1 tsp. salt
2 Tbs. margarine, melted	1/4 tsp. cinnamon, ground
1 Tbs. sugar	

Place carrots in a saucepan; cover with water. Cook until tender, about 8 or 10 minutes, and drain. Combine butter, sugar, salt and cinnamon; pour over carrots and toss to coat.

Candied Sweet Potatoes
Selected

3 to 4 lb. of sweet potatoes	1 stick margarine
1 c. white sugar	2 Tbs. flour
1 c. brown sugar	1 tsp. vanilla

Boil sweet potatoes, slice in halves and place in casserole dish. Bring to boil the remaining ingredients, except vanilla, then add vanilla after boiling. Pour over potatoes and bake at 350⁰ 30 min. or until syrup has thickened.

Fried Yams
Mary Fellure, Milton, FL

4 medium yams, peeled	4 Tbs. butter
1 qt. water	2 Tbs. sugar
1/2 tsp. salt	

Cut yams in 1 inch thick slices. Combine water and salt. Soak yam slices for 30 minutes. Remove from water, drain and pat dry. Melt butter in large frying pan until bubbly. Add yams and brown quickly on both sides. Sprinkle with sugar, stirring gently to coat both sides. Cover and reduce to low heat. Simmer for 15 to 20 minutes or until tender.

Harvard Beets

Selected

2 1/2 c. beets	1/4 c. vinegar
1/3 c. sugar	1/4 c. beet liquid
2 tsp. cornstarch	1 Tbs. margarine

Drain beets, reserving liquid. Combine sugar and cornstarch. Stir in vinegar and beet liquid. Stir over low heat until thickened; add beets and margarine and heat.

Pinto Bean Casserole

Selected

1 lb. hamburger (cooked)	1 tsp. chili powder
1/2 c. chopped onions	2 tsp. garlic salt
1 1/2 c. chopped tomatoes	Cornbread mixture
1 can pinto beans (or 2 c. cooked)	

Brown meat and sauté onions in mixture. Add other ingredients, except beans and simmer about 15 minutes. Add pinto beans and cover with 1 cup of cornbread mixture. Bake at 425⁰ for 20 more minutes or until cornbread is done.

Spanish Rice

Selected

2 c. uncooked instant rice	1 garlic clove, minced
1/4 c. margarine	1 medium onion, chopped
16 oz. tomatoes with liquid, cut up	1 tsp. sugar
1 c. boiling water	1 bay leaf
2 beef bouillon cubes	Salt & pepper to taste

In a saucepan over medium heat, melt margarine. Add rice and stir until browned. Add remaining ingredients and bring to a boil. Reduce heat, cover and simmer 15 minutes or until liquid is absorbed and rice is tender. Remove bay leaf before serving.

Fried Green Tomatoes

Selected

6 medium green tomatoes	1/2 tsp. salt
1/2 c. dry bread crumbs or flour	1/2 tsp. pepper

Wash and slice tomatoes. Coat your tomatoes in bread crumbs mixed with salt & pepper and brown on both sides in a small amount of oil.

Corn Stuffed Onions

Bonnie Pittman, Waycross, GA

6 medium onions	1/2 tsp. salt
12 oz. can of whole kernel corn, drained	Dash of pepper
	1 c. milk
2 Tbs. margarine	2 Tbs. chopped canned pimientos
2 Tbs. all purpose flour	4 oz. processed cheese, shredded

Hollow onions and chop centers to make 1 cup. Fill onions with corn; set aside remaining corn. Place onions in baking dish and add 2 Tbs. water; cover and bake at 400⁰ for 1 hour. Cook chopped onions in butter, stir in flour, salt & pepper. Add milk, remaining corn and pimientos. Return to boiling; stir in cheese until melted. Spoon sauce over onions.

Fried Okra

Selected

2 lbs. fresh okra	Salt & pepper to taste
1/2 c. cornmeal	App. 4 Tbs. oil

Wash okra and drain. Cut tips and slice across in 1/4 inch sections. Season slices with salt & pepper and roll in cornmeal. Fry in hot oil until tender and golden brown.

Fried Onion Rings
Selected

1/2 c. plain flour
1/2 tsp. baking powder
Salt to taste

1 egg, beaten
1/2 c. milk
Sliced onions

Mix flour, baking powder and salt. Add egg and milk to make a batter. Dip onion rings in batter and fry to crispy brown.

Macaroni and Cheese
Vicki Richburg, Six Mile, SC

1 1/2 c. uncooked macaroni
6 eggs, beaten
1 c. evaporated milk
1/2 c. milk

Salt & pepper to taste
1/2 lb. grated cheddar cheese
1 stick margarine

Cook and drain macaroni. Place in casserole dish. Mix eggs, milks, and seasonings and pour over macaroni and top with cheese. Cut up margarine and place over cheese. Bake at 350⁰ for 30 minutes till brown, but not dry.

The stomach is easier filled than the eye.
--German proverb

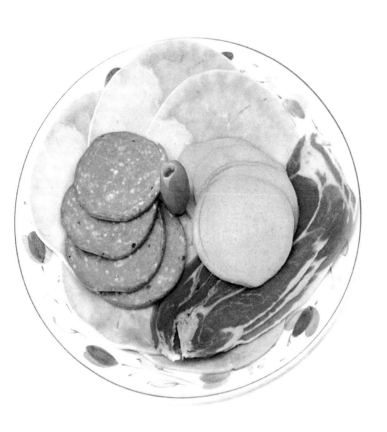

The eyes of all wait upon thee; and thou givest them their meat in due season. Psalm 145:15

Meats & Casseroles

Stuffed Peppers

Jennifer Fellure, Milton, FL

2 lb. ground beef	1 Tbs. sage
4 Tbs. onion, chopped	1 1/3 c. milk
1 egg	1/4 tsp. pepper
2 tsp. salt	2 c. toasted bread crumbs
1/4 tsp. dried mustard	6 bell peppers
or 2 tsp. prepared mustard	Catsup

Mix ingredients together, adding bread crumbs last. Cut off tops of green peppers and clean out insides. Stuff with meatloaf mixture. Cover with catsup. Bake 1 1/2 hours or until done at 350°.

Stuffed Bacon Burgers

Selected

1 1/2 lbs. ground beef	6 slices of American cheese
1 envelope dry onion soup mix	6 bacon strips
1/4 c. water	6 hamburger buns, toasted

In a bowl combine ground beef, soup mix and water. Mix well. Shape into 12 thin patties. Place a cheese slice on 6 of the patties and cover each with another patty. Pinch edges to seal. Wrap a strip of bacon around each: fasten with a wooden toothpick. Grill for 8 to 10 minutes, turning once or until desired doneness. Remove toothpicks and serve on buns.

Taco Bake

Selected

1 lb. ground beef	1 15 oz. can tomato sauce
1 small onion, chopped	1 pkg. shell macaroni, cooked &
3/4 c. water	drained
1 package taco seasoning	1 can green chilies (4 oz.)
2 c. shredded cheddar cheese, divided	

In a skillet brown ground beef and onion over medium heat; drain. Add the water, taco seasoning and tomato sauce. Bring to a boil, reduce heat and simmer for 20 minutes. Stir in macaroni, chilies and 1 1/2 c. of cheese. Pour into a greased casserole dish; sprinkle remaining cheese on top. Bake at 350° for 30 minutes or when heated thoroughly.

Basic Beef Roast

Selected

1 bottom round roast (3 1/2 lbs. or larger)
1 lg. onion, sliced
Salt & pepper to taste

Gravy:
1 Tbs. all purpose flour   2 c. water

Place beef, fat side up on a rack in a roasting pan. Season with salt and pepper; top with onion slices. Add enough water to pan to cover the bottom. Bake at 350^0 for 3 1/2 hours or until tender. For gravy; mix flour with water, stirring in pan drippings. Cook over medium heat until gravy has thickened.

Mozzarella Meat Loaf

Selected

2 lbs. lean ground beef   1/2 c. chopped onion
2 eggs, slightly beaten   1 1/2 tsp. salt
1 c. saltine crackers, crumbled 1 tsp. dried oregano
1 c. milk   1 can pizza sauce (8 oz.)
1/2 c. Parmesan cheese   3 slices of mozzarella cheese

Mix beef, eggs, cracker crumbs, milk, Parmesan cheese, onion, salt & oregano. Shape into a loaf and place in a loaf pan. Bake at 350^0 for 1 1/4 hours or until done. Drain. Spoon pizza sauce over loaf and top with mozzarella cheese. Return to oven for 10 minutes or until cheese melts.

Mushroom Burgers

Kate Cravatt, Brewton, AL

2 lbs. ground chuck formed   Water to be added
  into patties   1 - 4 oz. can mushroom pieces
1 can Campbell's Beefy   Swiss cheese (if desired)
  Mushroom Soup

Fry hamburger patties and drain. Arrange patties in skillet and add your Beefy Mushroom soup, mushrooms and water. Cover and simmer 1/2 hour. Use as hamburger on bun with Swiss cheese.

Broccoli Cheese Chicken

Betty Thomas, Greenville, NC

1 Tbs. margarine	1/3 c. water or milk
4 skinless, boneless	1/8 tsp. pepper
chicken breasts	2 c. broccoli flowerets
1 can Campbell's Broccoli	
Cheese soup	

In skillet over medium heat, melt margarine; fry chicken ten minutes or until browned on both sides. Drain off fat. Stir in soup, water and pepper. Heat to boiling and add broccoli. Reduce heat to low. Cover and simmer 10 minutes or until chicken is fork-tender and broccoli is done.

Breaded Chicken Breasts

Mary Fellure, Milton, FL

4 -6 boneless chicken breasts,	1/2 c. plain dry bread crumbs
halved	1 envelope Lipton Fiesta Herb &
3 Tbs. margarine, melted	Red Pepper soup mix

Preheat oven to 350⁰. Dip chicken in melted margarine, then in Lipton seasoning mix combined with bread crumbs. In 13 x 9 baking pan arrange chicken, drizzle with remaining margarine and bake 30 minutes or until done.

Stromboli

Letha Ray, Salt Rock, WV

1 lb. loaf Italian bread,	2 cloves garlic, minced
cut in half lengthwise	1/4 tsp. black pepper
1/2 lb. lean ground beef	1 c. prepared spaghetti sauce
1 medium onion, thinly sliced	1/4 c. mozzarella cheese, shredded
4 oz. mushrooms, thinly sliced	

In a Dutch oven brown beef and drain well. In same pan, sauté onion and mushroom with garlic and pepper. Stir in drained meat and spaghetti sauce. Heat until bubbly. Spread meat mixture over both halves of bread and top with cheese. Broil under low flame for 10 minutes.

Salisbury Steak

Letha Ray, Salt Rock, WV

1 can cream of mushroom soup	1 egg, beaten
1 lb. beef	1/4 c. minced onion
1/3 c. dried bread crumbs	1 1/2 c. sliced mushrooms

In a bowl mix thoroughly 1/2 cup of the soup, and the beef, bread crumbs, egg and onion. Shape firmly into 6 inch patties. In skillet over high heat, use 1 Tbs. hot oil and fry patties until brown. Spoon off fat. Stir in remaining soup and mushrooms. Return patties to skillet. Cover and simmer 20 minutes or until done.

Tuna Bake

Julie Waller, New Caney, TX

Small box of macaroni	1 can cream of mushroom soup
1 small onion, chopped	1 can of tuna
1 c. of grated cheese	Bread crumbs

Prepare macaroni; set aside. Sauté onion in butter. Now mix cooked macaroni, onion, soup and grated cheese; add tuna last. Top with bread crumbs and bake 20 minutes in 350⁰ oven.

Ground Beef and Noodle Casserole

Alma Schultz, Waycross, GA

1 green pepper (chopped)	1 - 8 oz. can of mushrooms
1 onion (chopped)	8 oz. noodles, cooked and drained
2 lb. ground round	8 oz. grated cheese (any yellow cheese)
2 - 16 oz. cans of tomatoes	

Brown green pepper and onion first; then brown meat. Add tomatoes, and mash them. Then add mushrooms and simmer all for 20 or 30 minutes. Then add the already cooked noodles. Put in large casserole dish and put grated cheese on top. The heat from mixture should melt the cheese

Taco Bake

Pat Mangus, Louisville, KY

2 lbs. ground beef
1 1/2 c. chopped onions
1 15 oz. can tomato sauce
1 can chopped green chilies
1 pkg. taco shells (or use nacho chips to line a 9 x 13 baking pan)

1 16 oz. can kidney or red beans
1 pkg. taco seasoning
Salt to taste
2 c. shredded cheese

Cook ground beef and onions, drain; stir in sauce, chilies, seasonings, and beans. Spoon mixture over shells, top with cheese. Bake at 350^0 for 15 -20 minutes until cheese melts. Serve with shredded lettuce, chopped tomatoes, and salsa or picante sauce.

Tamale Casserole

Pat Mangus, Louisville, KY

2 lbs. ground beef
1 c. onion, chopped
15 oz. tomato sauce
Nacho chips
16 oz. sm. curd cottage cheese

8 oz. sour cream
1 sm. can green chilies, chopped
2 c. cheddar cheese, grated
Black olives, sliced (Optional)

Brown ground beef with onion. Drain. Add tomato sauce and simmer while preparing the rest.

Layers:
1. Put a thin layer of crushed nacho chips on bottom of casserole.
2. Layer the meat and onion mixture.
3. Mix cottage cheese, sour cream and green chilies.
4. Grated cheddar cheese - amount depends upon the size of the casserole dish. (Black olives may be added.)
5. Top with crushed nacho chips.

Bake at 350^0 for 30 minutes or until cheese melts.

Tamale Pie

Norma Moore, Tyro, NC

1 1/2 lbs. hamburger
1 onion, chopped
1 green pepper, chopped
1 Tbs. salt & 1/2 Tbs. pepper
1 can Mexican chili beans
  or 1 1/2 c. leftover pintos

2 Tbs. cayenne pepper
1 can tomato soup
1 can corn, drained
Small box of Jiffy Cornmeal mix

Brown hamburger, onion, & pepper in skillet. Drain and rinse with water. Mix together all ingredients, place in casserole dish and top with small box of Jiffy cornmeal mix. Bake at 350⁰ until cornbread is brown, about 20 minutes.

Five Hour Stew

Brenda Rodgers, Milton, FL

1 1/2 to 2 lbs. stew meat
4 carrots
1 medium onion
4 or more potatoes

1 green pepper
2 celery stalks
Salt & pepper to taste
12 oz. V-8 juice

Cut all these into bite size pieces, sprinkle with salt and pepper. Place in shallow pan, cover with V-8 juice and cover with foil. Bake 5 hours at 250⁰.

Saucy Beef Over Rice

Brenda Rodgers, Milton, FL

1 Reynolds Oven Bag (large size)
2 Tbs. flour
14 1/2 oz.can stewed tomatoes
1 envelope onion soup mix

1/2 c. water
1/4 tsp. pepper
1 lb. beef sirloin steak
2 c. hot cooked rice

Bake at 350⁰. Shake flour in oven bag; place in 13 x 9 baking pan. Add undrained tomatoes, soup mix, water and pepper to bag. Squeeze the bag to blend together. Add cut up beef to bag. Turn bag and coat with sauce. Arrange ingredients in an even layer. Close bag with tie; cut slits in top. Bake until beef is tender, usually 40 - 50 minutes. Serve over rice.

Beef Tips With Rice
Norma Moore, Tyro, NC

1 lg. sirloin tip steak (cut in strips)
1 medium onion, chopped
1/2 stick margarine
2 Tbs. flour
1 can cream of chicken soup

1 Tbs. catsup
1 Tbs. Worcestershire sauce
1 c. water
1 small can sliced mushrooms

Brown sirloin tips and onion in butter. Add remaining ingredients and simmer 40 minutes.

Sausage & Sauerkraut
Carla Slutz, Franklin, TN

2 c. sauerkraut, drained
2 cooking apples, sliced thin
1/2 c. brown sugar

1 lb. smoked sausage, 3" pieces
2 tsp. prepared mustard
1 tsp. water

Mix saurkraut, apples and half of the sugar into a 1 1/2 qt. casserole. Arrange meat on top. Mix rest of brown sugar with mustard and water. Spread on meat. Bake at 400⁰ for 30 minutes.

Hamburger Pie
Mary Fellure, Milton, FL

1 lb. ground chuck
1 small onion (chopped)
1 can tomato sauce
1 can whole kernel corn

Salt & pepper to taste
Potatoes to mash
Cheddar cheese (Optional)

Brown ground meat and onion. Drain. Add tomato sauce and corn; simmer for approximately 30 miutes. While simmering, boil potatoes to mash. Place hamburger mixture in a casserole bowl and top with mashed potatoes. Note: Add cheese to top and melt, if desired.

Beef Pie

Norma Moore, Tyro, NC

1 1/2 lb. ground beef	1/4 tsp. garlic salt
1 medium onion, chopped	1 egg, well beaten
1 medium green pepper, chopped	1 can crescent dinner rolls
1 8 oz. can tomato sauce	1 or 2 pkgs. mozzarella cheese

Brown beef, onion, and pepper; add other ingredients, except rolls and cheese. In baking dish, line dinner rolls, pressing dough out. Pour mixture in dish. Add extra cheese to the top. Bake 20 to 25 minutes at 350⁰.

Sour Cream Casserole

Norma Moore, Tyro, NC

1 lb. hamburger	1 small carton sour cream
1 lg. onion, chopped	1 pkg. noodles
1/2 tsp. garlic powder	Grated cheese
1 small can tomato sauce	Salt & pepper to taste

Fry hamburger with onion. Drain. Add salt & pepper, garlic powder and tomato sauce. Simmer. Cook noodles and drain. Add sour cream to hamburger mixture. In casserole dish arrange noodles, then hamburger and top with cheese. Cover with tin foil. Bake at 350⁰ for 30 minutes.

Beef and Potato Casserole

Norma Moore, Tyro, NC

4 c. cooked ground beef	1/2 c. barbecue sauce
4 c. mashed potatoes	Salt & pepper, to taste
1 lg. onion, grated	3/4 c. grated cheese
2 eggs, beaten	1/2 c. catsup

Combine the ground beef, potatoes, onion, eggs, barbecue sauce, salt & pepper. Mix well. Press into casserole dish. Place cheese on top & pour catsup over the cheese. Cover and bake at 350⁰ for 20 minutes. Uncover and bake for 10 more minutes, then serve.

Chicken Parmesan

Norma Moore, Tyro, NC

4 to 6 chicken breasts	1 c. Parmesan cheese
2 c. bread crumbs	1 Tbs. garlic powder

Clean and skin chicken. Roll chicken in the remaining ingredients and bake in covered baking dish at 325° for 45 minutes or until chicken is tender.

Chicken & Dressing

Mary Fellure, Milton, FL

4 or 5 chicken breasts	1 can cream of chicken soup
Salt to taste	1/2 can water
1 pkg. Stove Top dressing, chicken flavor	

Boil chicken, cool and cut into parts. Prepare Stove Top dressing and add to chicken. Roll into balls (large as you like) and place in pan. Top with soup and water mixed. Bake in 350° oven 30 minutes or until soup is bubbling.

Chicken Divan

Maddy Ray, Tempe, AZ

2 10 oz. pkg. broccoli (or fresh spears)	1 tsp. lemon juice
6 - 8 chicken breasts or leftover turkey	1 tsp. curry powder
2 cans cream of chicken soup (undiluted)	1 c. grated cheese
3/4 c. mayonnaise	1/2 c. onion, chopped
	1/2 c. green chilies, chopped
	Buttered bread crumbs or crackers

Cook chicken and cut in bite size pieces. Cook broccoli & place in bottom of a buttered 13 x 9 pan. Mix soup, mayonnaise, juice, curry , cheese and other ingredients together well. Add chicken and put over broccoli. Cover with crumbs and bake 350° for 30 minutes.

Oven Pot Roast

Mary Fellure, Milton, FL

Large beef roast
2 pkgs. Lipton Onion Soup Mix

2 can cream of mushroom soup
2 can water

In a large, deep pan place onion soup mix in the bottom and place roast on top. Mix mushroom soup and water together and pour over roast. Cover and bake 3 or 4 hours at 300^0 or until tender.
Note: Be sure to turn roast and stir gravy mixture several times. If too thick, add more water.

Oven Roast

Norma Moore, Tyro, NC

Large pot roast
2 onions, quartered
2 Tbs. Worcestershire sauce

1 Tbs. teriyaki sauce
1 can golden mushroom soup
Salt & pepper to taste

Salt & pepper roast and place it and onions in pan lined with foil. Mix remaining ingredients and pour over roast. Cover with foil and bake at 350^0 for approximately 4 hours.

Easy Chicken Pie

Norma Moore, Tyro, NC

3 lb. frying chicken
1 can cream of chicken soup
1/2 c. margarine

2 c. chicken stock
1 c. self-rising flour
1 c. milk

Boil chicken until tender; debone and chop. Melt margarine in baking dish. Layer chicken in dish and pour soup and stock in. Mix flour and milk into a batter and pour over chicken. Bake at 350^0 for 1 hour.

Crescent Taco Bake
Selected

1 1/2 lbs. ground chuck	16 oz. sour cream
1 pkg. taco seasoning	8 oz. sharp cheddar cheese, grated
1 can crescent rolls	Lg. pkg. corn tortilla chips

Brown hamburger, drain and add taco seasoning. Line a 9 x 13 baking pan with crescent rolls. Crush half of chips on crescent rolls and then add hamburger mixture, sour cream, cheese and remaining chips, in the order given. Cover and bake 30 to 35 minutes at 350°.

Pepsi Chicken
Mary Fellure, Milton, FL

Clean and cut up whole chicken (10 or 12 pieces)	1 16 oz. catsup 1 16 oz. Pepsi or Dr. Pepper
Salt to taste	Opt. - 1 tsp. chilli powder
Flour to coat	

Mix Pepsi and catsup. Salt chicken to taste, coat with flour and add to catsup mixture. Cook very slowly on top of stove until done.

Lasagna
Jennifer Fellure, Milton, FL

1 lg. box lasagna noodles	1 lg. can of stewed tomatoes
1 1/2 lb. ground round	2 c. of mozzarella cheese
1 lg. can of tomato sauce	2 c. cheddar cheese
2 small cans of tomato paste	1 small can Parmesan cheese

Mix sauce, paste, and tomatoes together and let simmer. Brown meat and drain and mix with prepared sauce. Cook pasta noodles and drain. Layer meat-sauce, noodles, and cheese; repeat until pan is full. Bake at 350° for 30 to 40 minutes.

Make-Ahead Lasagna

Selected

1 lb. ground beef
1 envelope spaghetti sauce
  (Italian style)
2 - 6 oz. cans tomato paste
6 cans water

1/2 lb. lasagna noodles
12 oz. container of cottage cheese
8 oz. mozz. cheese, shredded
1/3 c. Parmesan cheese

Brown ground beef and drain. Add to the ground beef, spaghetti mix, tomato paste and water. Simmer 10 minutes. In a 13 x 9 pan spread 1 1/2 c. sauce; arrange layer of uncooked lasagna noodles; top with more sauce and some of each of the cheeses in layers. Repeat, making sure noodles are immersed in sauce. Refrigerate several hours or overnight. Bake in oven at 350⁰ for 45 minutes or until bubbly.

Easy Lasagna

Dorothy Grady, Mt. Olive, NC

1 1/2 lb. hamburger
1 pkg. meatloaf hamburger
  seasoning
3 - 8 oz. cans tomato sauce
1 c. water

8 oz. cheddar cheese, grated
8 oz. mozzarella cheese, sliced
8 oz. lasagna noodles, cooked
Salt & pepper to taste

Brown hamburger; salt & pepper to taste. Drain. Add to hamburger, meat loaf seasoning, tomato sauce and water. Simmer for 15 minutes. Layer in a baking dish: cooked noodles, 1/2 of sauce and 1/2 of both cheeses. Repeat layers of noodles, sauce and cheese. Bake for 20 minutes at 400⁰.

Easy Spaghetti Sauce

Selected

1 lb. ground beef
1 can tomato sauce
2 cans tomato paste
1/2 tsp. sweet basil

2 tsp. sugar
1/2 tsp. garlic
1 tsp. oregano
1 tomato sauce can of water

Brown beef, drain and add the ingredients. Cook slowly on stove for 2 hours.

Chicken Enchiladas

Jennifer Fellure, Milton, FL

2 c. cooked, chopped chicken
2 c. chicken broth
1 Tbs. flour
1 c. tomato puree
1 c. sour cream
1/2 tsp. oregano
1 tsp. salt
1/4 tsp. grd. cumin

1/4 tsp. chili powder
1 tsp. mashed garlic
1/2 c. chopped onion
2 c. milk
12 flour tortillas
Oil
1 1/2 c. grated Monterey Jack cheese

Microwave three chicken breasts on high for 10 minutes. Cool and chop into pieces. Add to chicken in large bowl: 1 c. chicken broth, flour, tomato puree, sour cream and all spices. Sauté garlic and onion a few minutes in butter and then add to mixture blend. Combine milk and 1 c. chicken broth in bowl. In fry pan, sauté flour tortilla in oil, just until hot (keep it soft). Dip them in milk mixture. Fill all tortillas with chicken filling and roll. After all are filled and rolled, place into 13 x 9 pan and pour remaining mixture over all. Top with grated cheese. Bake 20 minutes at 350⁰ until bubbly.

Chicken & Dressing Casserole

Maddy Ray, Tempe, AZ

4 lg. chicken breasts (save broth)
Salt & pepper for seasoning
Onion to taste
1 can cream of celery soup
1 can cream of chicken soup

1 c. milk
2 boxes Stove Top dressing
  (1 chicken, 1 corn bread)
Extra bread crumbs if needed

Stew chicken seasoned with salt & pepper until tender. Remove from bone and cut in bite size pieces. Place in bottom of a 9 x 13 baking pan. Chop onion (to taste) and sprinkle over the chicken. Mix soups and milk, pour over the chicken. Prepare stuffing (with 4 c. broth) and the 2 packets of seasoning. Use all the bread from the mixes, plus some extra. Spoon dressing over chicken & soups. Bake in 375⁰ oven until dressing is browned (approximately 25 - 30 minutes).
Note: 5 hot dog buns can be used for extra bread.

69

Skillet Lasagna
Selected

1 lb. ground beef
2 1/2 oz. pkg. spaghetti sauce mix
3 c. noodles, uncooked
1 tsp. salt
1 Tbs. basil

1 Tbs. parsley flakes
1 c. water
3 1/2 c. tomatoes
4 oz. mozzarella cheese, shredded

In crockpot or electric skillet, on high temperature, brown ground beef. Sprinkle spaghetti sauce mix over meat. Top with noodles and spices. Add tomatoes and water. Cover and reduce heat to medium. Cook 35 - 40 minutes. Remove, cover and sprinkle with cheese and let stand 10 to 15 minutes before serving.

Pork & Rice Balls
Beverly Roesch, DeFuniak Springs, FL

1 1/2 lbs. ground pork
1/2 c. uncooked rice
1/2 c. milk
1 Tbs. chopped green pepper
1 Tbs. chopped pimento

1 medium onion chopped
1 can tomato soup
1 can water
Salt & pepper to taste
Flour to coat

Mix all together, except soup and water. Form into balls and roll in flour. Put in baking dish. Pour soup and water mixture over all. Cover and bake about 1 1/2 hours at 350°.

Batter Dogs
Selected

1 c. pancake mix
1 Tbs. sugar
1/2 c. water

1 egg
1 pkg. weiners
Cooking oil

Mix together pancake mix, sugar, water and egg. Dip the wieners in the batter and fry in oil until golden brown.

Mexican Chicken

Ann Brown, Little Rock, AR

1 can cream of mushroom soup
2 cans cream of chicken soup
1 can Ro-Tel tomatoes
3/4 lb. Velveeta cheese, cut-up
1 Tbs. chili powder
1 lg. pkg. Doritos

1 c. chopped onions
1 c. chopped bell peppers
Green chilies, chopped
1/4 c. chicken broth
4 lg. chicken breasts (skinned, cooked
& deboned)

In skillet mix soups, Ro-tel tomatoes, cheese and chili powder. Heat until cheese is melted. In baking dish line with Doritos, sides and bottom. Make a layer of chicken, onions, peppers, and soup. Make another layer as above ending with soup on top. Pour 1/4 c. of chicken broth over top of casserole. Bake 325° for 30 minutes.

Crunchy Baked Chicken

Lillian Miller, Murfreesboro, TN

2 chicken breasts
1/2 c. corn flakes

1/2 c. skim milk

Preheat oven to 400°. Remove skin from chicken. Rinse and blot dry with a paper towel. Season to taste. Dip each piece in milk and then roll in crushed crumbs. Let stand briefly. Place chicken in oiled baking pan. Bake 45 minutes or until tender. Makes 2 servings

Jim's Spaghetti Sauce

Faye Chapman, Milton, WV

4 lbs. ground chuck, browned
3 onions, chopped
2   15 oz. cans of tomato sauce
4 small cans tomato paste
1 1/2 tsp. garlic powder
2 tsp. black pepper
4 tsp. salt

4 bay leaves
6 Tbs. chili powder
2 Tbs. vinegar
1 c. corn oil
3 c. water
1/4 c. sugar

Mix all ingredients and cook slowly for three hours. This makes good sauce for spaghetti or hot dogs.

Fried Chicken
Selected

1 fryer chicken (2 to 3 lbs.) cut-up 1/2 tsp. salt or more if desired
1 c. buttermilk   1/2 tsp. pepper or more if desired
1 c. all-purpose flour   Cooking oil

Place chicken in a large flat dish. Pour buttermilk over, cover and refrigerate for one hour. Combine flour, salt and pepper in a double-strength bag. Drain chicken pieces; toss one at a time in the flour mixture. Shake off excess, place on waxed paper for 15 minutes to dry. Heat oil in large skillet, fry chicken until browned on all sides. Cover and simmer, turning occasionally for 40 - 45 minutes, or until juices are clear and chicken is tender. Uncover and cook five minutes longer.

Shrimp Creole
Gladys Coker, New Caney, TX

1 lb. shrimp   2 cans tomato sauce
2 onions, chopped   1 tsp. chili
2 bell peppers, chopped   1 Tbs. Louisiana Red Hot sauce
1 garlic clove pod, chopped   1 Tbs. Worcestershire sauce
1 c. celery   Salt, pepper, & red pepper to taste
2 Tbs. oil

Heat oil, add onions, pepper, celery, garlic. Cook until clear, add tomato sauce and simmer 30 minutes. Add shrimp and cover. Cook on low 30 minutes.

Beef Stroganoff
Betty Simpson, San Antonio, TX

1 lb. cubed beef stew   1 pkg. Lipton mushroom soup
1 can cream of mushroom soup   1 can water

Mix and pour all ingredients in casserole dish. Bake at 350⁰ for approximately 1 1/2 hour. Serve over noodles or rice.

Steak and Gravy

Inez Rice, Picayune, MS

1 round steak, remove fat and cut up	1 c. milk
Flour to brown steak	1/2 c. water
Salt and pepper to season	1/2 c. flour

Coat steak with flour and season; put in casserole dish. Mix flour with milk and water, then pour over steak and bake covered for at least 1 hour at 375⁰.

Creole Rice Casserole

Donna Lisenbee, Boaz, AL

4 slices bacon	1 3/4 c. water
1 med. onion, chopped	8 oz. tomato sauce
1/2 c. chopped green pepper	2 tsp. chili powder
1 c. uncooked rice	1 tsp. salt
1 lb. hamburger meat	8 oz. shredded cheddar cheese
Garlic to taste	

Fry bacon crisp and crumble. Cook onion and green pepper in 2 tsp. bacon grease. Add rice and brown, stirring constantly. Add meat and garlic. Cook until lightly browned. Add water, tomato sauce, chili powder, salt. Heat to boiling, Cover, reduce heat and simmer for 20 minutes. Put half of rice mixture into casserole bowl. Sprinkle with 1/2 cheese and 1/2 bacon. Repeat layers. Bake at 450⁰ for 15 minutes.

Chinese Fried Rice

Norma Moore, Tyro, NC

1 lb. chicken, pork or shrimp	1 qt. cooked rice
2 Tbs. oil	1 egg, beaten
1 - 3 oz. can mushrooms, drained	Soy sauce to taste
1 1/2 Tbs. onion, chopped	

Fry meat in oil until done; add onion and mushrooms and cook 10 minutes. Add rice and soy sauce; cook a few more minutes. Stir in egg with a fork and cook again until done.

Shrimp Victoria

Donna Lisenbee, Boaz, AL

1 lb. shrimp, peeled & deveined
1/4 c. butter
1/2 c. onion, chopped
1 c. mushrooms, drained
1 Tbs. flour

1/4 tsp. salt
Dash of cayenne pepper
1 c. sour cream
1 1/2 c. cooked rice

Sauté shrimp and onion in butter for 5 minutes or until shrimp is tender.
Add mushrooms and cook 2 to 3 minutes more. Sprinkle in flour & spices.
Stir in sour cream and cook gently for 10 minutes being careful not to boil.
Serve over rice.

Easy Salmon Patties

Betty Thomas, Greenville, NC

1 can pink salmon
1 egg
1/3 c. minced onion

1/2 c. flour
1 1/2 tsp. baking powder
1 1/2 c. Crisco

Drain salmon; set aside 2 Tbs. of the juice. In a mixing bowl, mix salmon,
egg and onion until sticky. Stir in flour. Add baking powder to salmon juice
and stir into salmon mixture. Form into small patties and fry until golden
brown. Note: You may use flour to pat them in before frying.

Shrimp Spaghetti

Susan Taylor, Brunswick, GA

1 lb. cut up shrimp
1/2 stick butter or margarine
1 tsp. garlic salt
1 tsp. parsley
Black pepper to taste

1 small can of clams
1 bundle green onions
  (white part only, diced)
Spaghetti, cooked as usual
28 oz. can spaghetti sauce

Simmer shrimp in butter. Mix spices with clams and onion, while water for
spaghetti comes to a boil. Cook spaghetti. Mix together with sauce or pour
over spaghetti, if preferred.

74

Chinese Pepper Steak

Letha Ray, Salt Rock, WV

1 lb. sirloin steak, cut in strips
1 garlic clove, diced thin
2 green peppers, cut in rings
1 lg. sweet onion, cut in rings
2 stalks of celery, sliced thin

1 beef bouillon cube
Dash of soy sauce
2 Tbs. corn starch,
Water

Pour 1 Tbs. oil in wok. Heat on medium. Stir in garlic and mash well with back of spoon. Remove the garlic after a few seconds. Turn heat on high and add beef strips. Brown quickly stirring all the while; push to side of pan and add peppers, onion and celery. Continue to stir. Add 1/2 c. hot water in which 1 beef bouillon cube has been dissolved. Add a good dash of soy sauce. Cover and cook 5 minutes. Blend in 2 Tbs. corn starch and 1 Tbs. cold water. Add to ingredients in skillet and cook, stirring all the while until sauce is clear, 3 to 5 minutes. Serve over rice.

Spicy Mexican Rice

Selected

Vegetable cooking spray
1 tsp. oil
1/2 c. uncooked long grain rice
1/2 c. chopped onion
1 c. chopped tomatoes
1/3 c. chopped green pepper

1/4 tsp. garlic powder
1/4 tsp. ground red pepper
1/2 tsp. chili powder
1 tsp. bouillon granules
1 to 1 1/4 c. water

Coat a large skillet with cooking spray, add oil and place over medium heat. Add rice and onion; sauté about 3 minutes, stirring occasionally. Add remaining ingredients and bring to a boil. Cover, reduce heat and simmer for 25 minutes or until tender.

Baked Ham

Selected

Picnic ham
1 c. brown sugar

1 c. water
1/2 c. lemon juice

Place ham in baking bag. Mix other ingredients and pour over. Bake at 350⁰ for 1 1/2 to 2 hours.

Baked Spaghetti
Selected

1 c. chopped onion
1 c. chopped green pepper
1 Tbs. butter
1 can (28 oz.) tomatoes with liquid
1 small can mushrooms, drained
1 small can sliced ripe olives,
  drained
2 tsp. dried oregano

1 lb. ground beef, browned & drained
12 oz. spaghetti, cooked & drained
2 c. shredded cheddar cheese
1 can cream of mushroom soup,
  undiluted
1/4 c. water
1/4 c. grated Parmesan cheese

In a large skillet, sauté onion and green pepper in butter until tender. Stir in tomatoes, mushrooms, olives and oregano. Add ground beef. Simmer, uncovered for 10 minutes. Place half of the spaghetti in a greased 13 x 9 in. baking dish. Top with half of the vegetable mixture. Sprinkle with 1 cup of cheddar cheese. Repeat layers. Mix the soup and water until smooth; pour over casserole. Sprinkle with Parmesan cheese. Bake uncovered at 350^0 for 30 - 35 minutes.

Barbecued Chicken in the Oven
Selected

2 1/2 to 3 lb. chicken, halved
Salt, black pepper & red pepper
Butter

Worcestershire sauce
Barbecue sauce

Preheat oven to 350^0. Wash and split chicken in halves. Season well. Refrigerate overnight. Melt butter in saucepan, add 1 tablespoon of Worcestershire sauce and mix well. Brush mixture on chicken halves, both sides. Place chicken halves, skin side on baking sheet, for one hour or until well cooked. Turn chicken over, brush with barbecue sauce and bake 5 to 10 minutes longer. Repeat with barbecue sauce. Bake a few minutes longer.

Golden Glazed Chicken
Vicki Richburg, Six Mile, SC

2 - 3 lbs. chicken, cut-up
1 pkg. dry onion soup

1 bottle Russian dressing
1 small bottle apricot preserves

Mix soup, dressing and preserves in small bowl. Arrange cleaned chicken with thickest pieces to the outside of baking dish. Cover each piece with sauce. Cook, covered with wax paper in microwave on high 18 to 22 minutes, rotating dish after 10 minutes. Let stand 5 to 10 minutes before serving.

Cheesy Chicken Wings
Susan Taylor, Brunswick, GA

16 chicken wings
3/4 c. fine bread crumbs
1/2 tsp. salt
1 tsp. dried basil leaves

1/2 tsp. dried oregano leaves
3/4 c. Parmesan cheese
2 Tbs. butter or margarine

Wash chicken wings, pat dry. In a bowl, combine the bread crumbs, herbs and Parmesan cheese. Add seasonings and mix well to blend. Melt butter. Dip chicken wings, first in melted butter, then into crumb coating. Arrange chicken wings in lightly oiled ovenproof baking dish. Bake chicken wings at 375^0 for about 30 minutes or until lightly brown and done. Chicken wings should be tender.

Barbecued Chicken
Geraldine Chapman, Brunswick, GA

2 1/2 or 3 lbs. fryer, cut up
1 c. catsup
1 c. water
3 Tbs. Worcestershire sauce
3 Tbs. brown sugar
1/2 tsp. salt

1/2 tsp. pepper
1/4 c. lemon juice
1 tsp. prepared mustard
1/8 tsp. hot sauce (opt.)
1/2 c. celery, chopped (opt.)

Place chicken in baking dish. Mix remaining ingredients for sauce and bring to a boil. Pour over chicken and bake in oven at 400^0 for 1 to 1 1/4 hour or until tender. Good served with rice or noodles.

Chicken Casserole

Barbara Rogerson, Goose Creek, SC

4 lg. chicken breasts	1 can cream of mushroom soup
1 stick margarine	1 can cream of chicken soup
1 pkg. Pepperidge Farm	Water
Cornbread dressing	

Boil chicken breasts until done. (Do not use salt.) Save broth. Cut chicken in bite size pieces. Melt butter and stir into dressing. In a 13 x 9 greased baking dish, put a layer of dressing, a layer of chicken then a layer of mushroom soup, diluted with a can of broth. Again a layer of dressing, chicken, and can of chicken soup, diluted with water. Top with dressing and bake at 350⁰ for 45 minutes.

Shrimp Almandine

Betty Thomas, Greenville, NC

1/2 c. slivered almonds	1/2 tsp. dillweed
2 Tbs. margarine	1/2 tsp. salt
3/4 lb. medium shrimp	1/4 tsp. pepper
1 can chicken broth (13 1/4 oz)	1 1/2 c. dried minute rice
1 10 oz. pkg. frozen green peas	1/2 c. pimentos
with pearl onions	

Sauté almonds in butter until lightly browned. Add shrimp and sauté about five minutes until shrimp is pink. Add broth, vegetables and seasonings. Bring to a full boil. Stir in rice and pimentos. Cover and remove from heat. Let stand for five minutes. Fluff with fork.

Meat Loaf

Betty Thomas, Greenville, NC

1 can cream of mushroom soup	2 Tbs. chopped parsley
2 lbs. ground beef	1 Tbs. Worcestershire sauce
1/2 c. fine dried bread crumbs	1 egg, slightly beaten
1/2 c. chopped onions	Salt & pepper to taste

Mix all ingredients thoroughly. Shape firmly into loaf pan. Bake at 350⁰ for 1 1/4 hours.

Chili
Selected

2 lb. ground beef	1 c. water
1 lg. onion, chopped	1 tsp. chili powder
1 pkg. chilli mix	1 pkg. dried onion soup
1 large can tomatoes	2 cans of kidney beans, drained
1 small can of tomatoes	

Brown meat and onion together. Drain. Add chili mix, water, and tomatoes. Sprinkle on chili powder and onion soup. Add kidney beans. Heat on low heat until cooked thoroughly.

Saucy Meat Loaf
Norma Moore, Tyro, NC

1 1/2 lbs. ground beef	1/2 c. chopped onion
3/4 c. Quaker oats, quick	1 egg, beaten
1 1/2 tsp. salt	3/4 c. milk
1/4 tsp. pepper	

Combine all ingredients. Pack into loaf pan. Spread with topping (below). Bake about 1 hour at 350⁰.

Topping:

1/3 c. catsup	1 Tbs. prepared mustard
1 Tbs. brown sugar	

Ham Casserole
Donna Lisenbee, Boaz, AL

10 oz. frozen chopped broccoli	1 c. cooked rice
1 c. cheddar cheese soup	1/2 c. sour cream
1 c. tender chunk ham	1/2 c. buttered bread crumbs
(Opt. chicken or turkey)	

Preheat oven to 350⁰. Cook broccoli until tender, drain. Stir in soup and sour cream. Combine all ingredients and sprinkle with bread crumbs. Bake 30 to 35 minutes.

Ham and Broccoli Casserole

Lois Dixon, San Antonio, TX

4 Tbs. margarine
4 Tbs. flour
2 c. whole milk
8 oz. sharp cheddar cheese
1 tsp. onion powder

1 tsp. garlic powder
1/2 tsp. pepper
1 lb. left over ham slices
1 lb. broccoli, steamed and cut

Preheat oven to 350°. Melt margarine in fry pan; add flour. Stir to blend. Add milk and cook until thickened. Remove from heat and add cheese, onion powder, garlic powder and black pepper. Stir until cheese is melted. In oven proof dish, layer first ham slices then the broccoli and top with cheese sauce. Bake for 30 minutes until heated. Serves 6 - 8.

Fancy Franks

Jennifer Fellure, Milton, FL

1 small jar mustard
1 small jar current jelly

2 lbs. frankfurters

Melt jelly and mustard. Cut franks into 1 inch pieces. Cover and simmer for 20 to 25 minutes. Serve on toothpicks.

Barbecued Pork Chops

Selected

10 boneless pork chops
1/2 c. brown sugar
2 Tbs. vinegar
2 c. catsup

2 Tbs. Worcestershire sauce
1 Tbs. paprika
Salt & pepper to taste

Mix all ingredients together. Pour over pork chops and bake in a covered dish for 1 hour or until done at 375°.

Stir Fry

Selected

1 lb. stew meat
1 Tbs. oil
1 Tbs. soy sauce

1 - 10 oz. pkg. mixed vegetables
1/4 c. water

Heat oil and soy sauce in wok. Add meat and sauté over high heat until done. Push meat to the side and add water and vegetables. Reduce heat, cover and simmer until vegetables are tender.

Cheeseburger Loaf

Madeline Darnell, Sulphur, LA

1 can cream of mushroom soup
2 lbs. ground beef
1/2 c. fine dry bread crumbs
1 onion, chopped
1 Tbs.Worcestershire sauce

1 egg, beaten
1 tsp. salt
Pepper to taste
1/2 c. shredded cheese

Mix soup, ground beef, bread crumbs, onion, Worcestershire sauce, egg, salt and pepper. Mix thoroughly; shape firmly in loaf. Place in shallow pan and bake at 350⁰ for 1 hour. Top with cheese and bake 1 minute more.

Ground Beef and Cabbage Casserole

Selected

1 1/2 lb. ground beef
1 can Ro-Tel tomatoes
3 c. rice, cooked
1/3 c. oil
1 lg. onion, chopped

1 medium cabbage head, finely
  chopped
1 lg. green pepper, chopped
5 dashes Tabasco sauce

Mix all ingredients well. Place in a greased casserole dish. Bake at 325⁰ for about 35 minutes.

Barbecue Sauce for Spareribs
Sonya Greer, Loveland, OH

Spareribs	2 Tbs. Worcestershire sauce
2 med. onions	1 tsp. salt
3/4 c. catsup	1 tsp. paprika
3/4 c. water	1 tsp. chili powder .
3 Tbs. vinegar	1/4 tsp. black pepper

Place meat in skillet, slice onions and lay them on top of meat. Combine remaining ingredients and pour over onions. Cook on stovetop on medium heat 2 hours or till meat is thoroughly done.

Sloppy Joes
Norma Moore, Tyro, NC

1 lb. ground beef	1/2 c. catsup
1/2 c. chopped onion	1 tsp. salt
1/2 c. chopped celery	1 tsp. pepper
1 can condensed tomato soup	6 hamburger buns

Brown hamburger adding onion and celery. Drain. Add remaining ingredients and cook until heated thoroughly. Spoon on buns and top with cheese.

Turkey Tetrazzini
Vicki Richburg, Six Mile, SC

1 box (7 oz.) spaghetti, broken	1/3 c. milk
2 c. cooked turkey, chopped	1/4 c. green pepper, chopped
1 c. cheddar cheese	2 oz. chopped pimentos
1 can cream of mushroom soup	Salt & pepper to taste
1 medium onion, chopped	Top with extra cheese
2 4 oz. can mushrooms, drained	

Cook spaghetti as directed on package. Drain. In large bowl, add the remaining ingredients, except cheese for top, and mix well. Transfer to greased baking dish and top with cheese. Bake uncovered at 375° for 45 minutes or until heated thoroughly.

The way to a man's heart is through his stomach.

-- Spanish proverb

Delight thyself also in the LORD; and he shall give thee the desires of thine heart. Psalms 37:4

CAKES
Scripture Cake

Selected

1 c. butter (Judges 5:25)	1 tsp. salt (Leviticus 2:13)
2 c. sugar (Jeremiah 6:20)	1/2 c. milk (Judges 4:19)
2 Tbs. honey (I Samuel 14:25)	2 c. raisins (I Samuel 30:12)
6 eggs (Jeremiah 17:11)	2 c. dried figs (Nahum 3:12)
4 1/2 c. flour (I Kings 4:22)	2 c. almonds (Numbers 17:8)
2 tsp. baking powder (Amos 4:5)	
1/2 tsp. (each) nutmeg, allspice,	
& cinnamon (II Chronicles 9:9)	

Cream butter, sugar and honey. Add eggs one at a time, beating well after each. Combine flour, baking powder, salt and spices. Blend butter mixture alternately with milk. Stir in raisins, figs and almonds. Bake in greased and floured 12 c. tube pan for 40 to 50 minutes on 350^0.

German Chocolate Cake

Ann Brown, Little Rock, Arkansas

1 German chocolate cake mix	3 or 4 Heath candy bars
1 lg. Cool Whip	1 bottle caramel topping
1 can Eagle Brand milk	1/2 c. chopped almonds

Bake cake (follow package directions). Punch holes in cake, while it is still warm, pour Eagle Brand over cake. Let cake cool. Spread caramel over top of cake. Spread Cool Whip over caramel. Sprinkle chopped almonds on top. Sprinkle chopped Heath bars over that, then add a few more almonds.

Kate's Cheese Cake

Kate Cravatt, Brewton, AL

8 oz. graham cracker crust	1 tsp. vanilla
8 oz. cream cheese (softened)	Sugar to taste (I use 3 or 4 tsp.)
4 oz. Cool Whip	

Mix softened cream cheese and Cool Whip; add vanilla and sugar. Pour into graham cracker crust and chill. Top with favorite fruit or crumbled Oreo cookies.

83

German Chocolate Upside-Down Cake

Amanda Doyle, Groveton, TX

Spray oblong (9 x 13) pan with Pam and sprinkle bottom of pan with:

1 c. chopped pecans   1 c. angel flake coconut

Mix 1 pkg. German chocolate cake mix as directed. Pour over pecans and coconut.

Filling (Mix well with mixer.)
2 c. powdered sugar   1 stick of margarine
1 8 oz. cream cheese

Drop by teaspoonful over cake mixture. Bake 45 minutes at 350⁰. Note: The cake will cook around filling. Turn out on cake plate when cooled.

Cream Cheese Cake

Mina Sims, San Antonio, TX

8 oz. cream cheese, softened   5 eggs
3 sticks butter   3 c. flour
3 c. sugar   1 tsp. vanilla

Cream butter and cheese until fluffy; add sugar gradually. Then add eggs, one at a time; then flour and vanilla. Bake at 350⁰ for 1 hour and 15 minutes.

Chocolate Mayonnaise Cake

Rosella Rowe, Lexington, NC

2 c. all-purpose flour   1 c. mayonnaise
1 tsp. baking soda   1 c. sugar
1/4 tsp. salt   1 c. water
1/4 c. cocoa

In a medium mixing bowl, sift flour, baking soda, salt and cocoa. In another mixing bowl beat sugar, mayonnaise, and water until fluffy; add mixture to flour mixture and bake at 350⁰ for 35 minutes. This cake is best baked in a 9 x 13 pan.

German Sweet Chocolate Cake

Ruby Pickens, Canton, NC

1 c. butter	1 cake German sweet chocolate
2 c. sugar	1/2 c. boiling water
4 eggs, separated	2 tsp. vanilla
1 tsp. baking soda	1/8 tsp. salt
1 c. sour milk	2 1/2 c. flour

Cream butter and sugar. Add egg yolks one at a time. Beat well. Dissolve soda in small amount of sour milk. Melt chocolate in 1/2 c. boiling water. Add to creamed butter and sugar. Beat well. Add sour milk alternately with flour mixed with salt. Add vanilla. Last add beaten egg whites, by hand. Bake at 350⁰ for 25 minutes or until done. Makes 3 layers.

Punch Bowl Cake

Inez Rice, Picayune, MS

1 box yellow cake mix	1 small can crushed pineapple
1 lb. fresh or frozen strawberries	1 - 3 oz. instant vanilla pudding
3 or 4 bananas	1 - 12 oz. Cool Whip

Bake two layers of cake at 350⁰ for 30 minutes. Put one layer of cake in a punch bowl or large bowl, then half of: pineapple, strawberry, banana and pudding mixture. Then put the other layer of cake and repeat fruit ingredients. Spread Cool Whip on top.

Earthquake Cake

Jennifer Fellure, Milton, FL

1 c. chopped pecans	1 stick margarine, softened
1 c. shredded coconut	8 oz. cream cheese, softened
1 box German chocolate cake mix	1 lb. confectioners sugar

Grease and flour 9 x 13 cake pan. Spread pecans and coconut evenly on bottom of pan. Mix cake mix as directed on package. Pour cake batter over coconut and pecans. Mix together butter, cream cheese and confectioners sugar. Spoon this mixture by spoonfuls over cake batter. Bake at 350⁰ for 45 - 50 minutes. Cake will be a little soft, but will set up.

Creamy Pound Cake

Mary Fellure, Milton, FL

1 c. butter or margarine	1 tsp. butternut flavoring
1/3 c. shortening (Crisco)	1/2 tsp. baking powder
3 c. sugar	3 c. flour
6 eggs	1 c. milk
1 tsp. vanilla	

Cream butter and shortening. Add sugar gradually and cream well. Add eggs one at a time and beat well after each. Add flavorings and baking powder. Add flour, alternating with milk until flour disappears. Start with cold oven and bake 1 hour and 15 minutes at 325⁰.

Buttermilk Pound Cake

Mary Fellure, Milton, FL

2 1/2 c. sugar	3 c. flour
1 1/2 c. Crisco	1/2 tsp. salt
6 eggs	1/2 tsp. soda
1 tsp. vanilla	1 c. buttermilk
1 tsp. lemon flavoring	

Cream sugar and Crisco well. Add eggs one at a time. Add flavorings. Mix dry ingredients together and add alternately with buttermilk. Bake at 300⁰ for 1 1/2 to 2 hours.

Jell-O Pound Cake

Selected

1 box yellow or lemon cake mix	2/3 c. oil
1 box lemon instant Jell-O	2/3 c. water
4 eggs	

Mix all ingredients and beat 4 minutes. Pour into greased and floured tube pan. Bake at 350⁰ for 45 to 50 minutes. Remove from pan and cool.

Lowfat Carrot Cake

Madeline Darnell, Sulphur, LA

4 c. grated carrots	2 tsp. soda
2 c. sugar	1/2 tsp. salt
8 oz. can crushed pineapple	2 tsp. cinnamon
1 c. prune puree **	2 c. flour
4 lg. egg whites	3/4 c. coconut
2 tsp. vanilla	

In a large bowl, combine carrots, sugar, pineapple, prune puree, egg whites and vanilla; blend thoroughly. Add remaining ingredients, except coconut; mix completely. Gently stir in coconut. Spread in 9 x 13 pan (greased and floured). Bake at 375⁰ for 45 minutes or until done. **Prune Puree: Combine 1 1/3 c. pitted prunes and 6 Tbs. water in food processor. Pulse on and off until prunes are finely chopped. Makes 1 cup.

Oreo Delight

Selected

1 small pkg. Oreo cookies	2 pkg. vanilla instant pudding
1 (8 oz.) Cool Whip	4 c. milk
1 (8 oz.) cream cheese, softened	

Crumble 1/2 of the Oreos in a dish. Mix pudding and milk in a bowl. In another bowl, mix Cool Whip and cream cheese well. Mix all together and pour over cookie crumbs. Crumble rest of cookies and sprinkle over top.

Dump Cake

Maddy Ray, Tempe, AZ

1 can 20 oz. crushed pineapple & syrup	1 pkg. Duncan yellow cake mix
1 can 21 oz. cherry pie filling	1 c. pecans
	1/2 c. butter cut in thin slices

Heat oven to 350⁰. Grease 13 x 9 pan. Dump pineapple in pan; spread evenly. Dump pie filling; spread evenly. Dump dry cake mix on cherry filling, evenly. Sprinkle pecans. Put butter on top. Bake 48 - 53 minutes.

Cream Cheese Carrot Cake
Amanda Doyle, Groveton, TX

1 (8 oz.) cream cheese, softened
1/4 c. sugar
1 tsp. vanilla

1 egg
1 box carrot cake mix
1/2 c. walnuts

Heat oven to 350⁰. Grease and flour pan (9 x 13). Beat cream cheese, sugar, vanilla and egg in small bowl on medium speed until smooth; reserve. Prepare cake batter as directed on package. Pour batter into pan. Spoon cream cheese mixture by generous tablespoon randomly in 10 or 12 mounds onto batter, not touching sides of pan. Swirl cream cheese mixture. Sprinkle with walnuts. Bake 35 to 40 minutes.

No Bake Cake
Selected

1 prepared angel food cake
1 can crushed pineapple
30 large marshmallows

1 c. milk
2 envelopes of whipped topping
3 1/2 oz. coconut

Crumble cake and spread evenly in bottom of a large oblong pan. Pour pineapple evenly over cake. Heat milk and marshmallows in saucepan over low heat until marshmallows are melted. Pour evenly over layer of pineapples. Prepare whipped topping and spread over cake. Sprinkle with coconut.

Turtle Cake
Maddy Ray, Tempe, AZ

1 box German chocolate cake mix
1 14 oz. pkg. of caramels
1/2 c. evaporated milk

3/4 c. margarine
2 c. chopped pecans
1 c. chocolate chips

Mix cake mix according to package. Pour 1/2 of the batter into greased 9 x 13 pan. Bake for 15 minutes at 350⁰. Melt caramels, margarine and milk together. Pour over the cake and sprinkle the pecans and chocolate chips on top. Pour the remaining batter over the mixture and bake for 20 minutes at 350⁰.

Chocolate Trifle

Leona Callaway, Milton, FL

1 pkg. chocolate fudge cake mix
1/2 c. strong coffee
1 pkg. instant chocolate pudding
mix

12 oz. frozen whipped topping
6 Heath or Milky Way bars, crushed

Bake cake; let cool. Make pudding and set aside. Crumble cooled cake; reserve 1/2 c. for top. Place half crumbled cake in a large bowl; layer with half of coffee, pudding, whipped topping and half crushed candy bars. Repeat with remaining cake, coffee, pudding and whipped topping. Combine remaining candy with 1/2 c. reserved cake crumbs, sprinkle on top. Refrigerate 4 to 5 hours.

Thrifty Pound Cake

Maddy Ray, Tempe, AZ

Mix together:
3 c. flour
1/2 tsp. soda

1/2 tsp. baking powder
3/4 tsp. salt

Beat 2 1/2 minutes in a large bowl:
1 c. butter or shortening
2 c. sugar
4 eggs, unbeaten

1 tsp. vanilla
1 tsp. lemon

Add flour mixture alternately with 1 c. buttermilk and beat 2 1/2 minutes more. Bake at 350^0 for 1 hour and 10 min.

Mamie's Pound Cake

Barbara Countryman, Milton, FL

1 1/3 c. butter or margarine
2 1/2 c. sugar
6 eggs
1/2 tsp. baking soda

1/3 c. buttermilk
3 c. sifted flour
2 Tbs. lemon flavoring

Cream butter and sugar; add eggs, one at a time. Put soda in buttermilk. Alternate buttermilk and flour with sugar mixture. Add flavoring. Bake at 350^0 for 1 1/4 hours. Test: Cook longer if necessary.

Snowball Cake

Mary Fellure, Milton, FL

2 pkg. Knox gelatin	3 pkg. Dream Whip
4 Tbs. cold water	1 c. milk
1 c. sugar	1 c. pineapple (drained)
1 c. pineapple juice or 1 lemon	Large angel food cake
1 c. hot water	Coconut

Dissolve gelatin in 4 Tbs. cold water. Add 1 c. sugar, 1 c. pineapple juice and 1 c. hot water. Place in refrigerator to jell. Whip 2 pkgs. of Dream Whip in 1 c. milk. Add drained pineapple. Break cake in small pieces and cover bottom of pan. Mix Dream Whip with gelatin mixture. Put in layers with cake until all is used up. Now whip 1 pkg. Dream Whip and spread over cake. Sprinkle generous amount of coconut on top. Let set in refrigerator overnight.

Chocolate Chip Cheesecake

Selected

1 1/2 c. graham cracker crumbs	1 can sweetened condensed milk
1/3 c. Hershey's Cocoa	3 eggs
1/2 c. sugar	2 tsp. vanilla extract
1/3 c. margarine, melted	1 tsp. all-purpose flour
3 - 8 oz. pkgs. cream cheese	
1 c. Hershey's mini chips semisweet chocolate, divided	

Heat oven to 300⁰. In bowl, combine graham cracker crumbs, cocoa, sugar and butter; press evenly onto bottom of 9 inch springform pan. In large mixer bowl, beat cream cheese until fluffy. Gradually add sweetened condensed milk, beating until smooth. Add eggs and vanilla, mix well. In small bowl, toss 1/2 c. mini chips with flour to coat. Stir into cheese mixture. Pour into prepared pan. Sprinkle remaining chips evenly over top. Bake 1 hour. Turn oven off and allow to cool in oven 1 hour. Remove from oven, cool to room temperature. Refrigerate before serving. Cover. Refrigerate left over cheesecake.

Waldorf Red Cake
Maddy Ray, Tempe, AZ

1/2 c. shortening	1 c. buttermilk
1 1/2 c. sugar	2 1/4 c. flour
2 eggs	1 tsp. vanilla
2 oz. red food coloring	1 Tbs. vinegar
2 Tbs. cocoa	1 tsp. baking soda
1 tsp. salt	

Cream shortening, sugar and eggs. Make paste with coloring and cocoa. Add to mixture. Add salt and buttermilk with flour and vanilla. Add vinegar and soda. Bake 30 minutes at 350^0.

Chocolate Cherry Ring Cake
Carla Slutz, Franklin, PA

2 c. flour	1/2 c. canola oil
3/4 c. sugar	1 tsp. vanilla
1 tsp. baking soda	1 21 oz. can cherry pie filling
1 tsp. cinnamon	1 c. chocolate pieces
1/8 tsp. salt	1 c. chopped walnuts
2 beaten eggs	Powdered sugar for top

In a large mixing bowl, stir together flour, sugar, baking soda, cinnamon and salt. In another bowl combine eggs, oil and vanilla: Add to flour mixture. Mix well. Stir in cherry pie filling, chocolate pieces and nuts. Turn cherry mixture into a greased and floured 10 inch fluted tube pan. Bake in a 350^0 oven for 1 hour. Cool on pan in a wire rack for 15 minutes. Remove from pan and cool; sift powdered sugar on top.

Ice Box Fruit Cake
Norma Moore, Tyro, NC

12 lg. or 60 small marshmallows	16 oz. vanilla wafers (rolled fine)
1 can condensed milk	1 lb. cut-up red cherries
4 c. pecans, chopped	1 lg. box dates, cut-up

Mix all ingredients and make a roll. Wrap in aluminum foil and refrigerate.

Seven-Up Cake

Donna Ray, Venice, FL

Cake:

1 box yellow cake mix
4 eggs
1 box pineapple or vanilla instant pudding
3/4 c. Wesson oil
10 oz. 7-Up

Beat all ingredients together, except 7-Up. Add it last and beat well. Bake in 13 x 9 pan for 40 minutes in 350° oven.

Icing:

2 eggs, beaten
1/2 c. sugar
1 Tbs. flour
1 stick butter
1 c. crushed pineapple (undrained)
1 can coconut

Cook the above ingredients except coconut until thick; then add the coconut and pour over hot cake.

Cream Cheese Cake

Donna Ray, Venice, FL

Crust:

6 Tbs. melted oleo
1 2/3 c. crushed graham crackers
1 1/2 tsp. cinnamon

Mix and line bottom of glass pan.

Filling:

3 - 8 oz. pkgs. cream cheese, softened
3 large eggs
1 c. sugar

Cream together, pour into crust and bake at 350° for 25 minutes.

Topping:

1 pt. sour cream
3 tsp. sugar
1 tsp. vanilla

Mix and pour over filling evenly; spread with rubber spatula. Return to oven; bake at 450° for 5 minutes.

Four Layer Dessert

Barbara Freeman, Texarkana, AR

Melt 2 sticks margarine and add 2 c. of flour & 1 c. chopped nuts. Spread in 13 x 9 baking pan. Bake about 15 minutes at 375⁰. Cool.

Mix an 8 oz. package cream cheese with 1 c. powdered sugar and 1 c. Cool Whip. Spread on cooled crust. Chill.

Mix 2 small packages of instant pudding with 3 c. milk until smooth. Spread on cream cheese mixture.

Cover top with 2 more cups of Cool Whip. Sprinkle with more chopped nuts. Keep in refrigerator.

Pea Picking Cake

Barbara Countryman, Milton, FL

Cake:
1 box golden yellow or butter cake mix
1 small can mandarin oranges with juice
4 eggs
1/2 c. oil

Beat all ingredients together until well blended. Put cake batter into three greased and floured cake pans. Bake at 350⁰ about 25 minutes.

Filling:
1 lg. container Cool Whip
20 oz. can crushed pineapple with juice
1 small box vanilla pudding (instant)

Combine crushed pineapple and juice with box of instant pudding. Fold Cool Whip into this mixture. Spread between and on top of three layers of cake. Refrigerate overnight.

Zucchini Bread Cake

Betty White, Belleville, MI

3 eggs	2 tsp. soda
1 c. oil	1 tsp. salt
1 tsp. vanilla	3/4 tsp. nutmeg
2 c. sugar	1 1/2 tsp. cinnamon
8 oz. crushed pineapple & juice	2 c. shredded zucchini
3 c. flour	1 c. raisins
1/2 tsp. baking powder	1 c. chopped walnuts

Mix together eggs, oil, vanilla, sugar and pineapple with juice. Then add dry ingredients. Stir in zucchini, raisins and nuts. Bake at 350° for 50 - 60 minutes. This makes 2 or 3 loaves.
Note: Spray pans with Pam.

Apple Shortcake

Beverly Roesch, DeFuniak Springs, FL

2 c. flour	1 c. margarine
2 tsp. baking powder	3/4 c. milk
1/2 tsp. salt	1 egg
1/8 tsp. cinnamon	2 lg. apples sliced
1/8 tsp. nutmeg	1 Tbs. sugar
1 c. brown sugar	

Mix all dry ingredients in large bowl. Stir in brown sugar and cut in 6 Tbs. margarine until mixture is crumbly. Save 1/2 c. mixture. Break egg into cup and add milk to make 1 cup liquid. Stir into flour mixture and pour into greased pie plate. Arrange apple slices in circle. Top with 1/2 c. crumb mixture. Dot with butter and sprinkle with sugar. Bake at 350° for 45 minutes. Serve hot with ice cream.

Apple Dapple Cake

Vicki Richburg, Six Mile, SC

Cake:

1 1/2 c. vegetable oil	1 tsp. salt
2 c. sugar	2 tsp. vanilla
3 eggs	3 c. peeled & sliced apples
3 c. all purpose flour	1 c. each coconut, raisins, &
1 tsp. baking soda	pecans or walnuts

Cream oil, sugar and eggs; add remaining ingredients stirring well. Turn into a greased & floured tube pan and bake in preheated oven for 1 hour and 25 minutes at 325^0.

Topping:

1 c. brown sugar	1/4 c. milk
1 stick margarine	

Bring to boil and pour over warm cake. Allow to stand 5 minutes, then spoon remaining sauce over cake

Tennessee Mud Cake

Beulah Potts, Milton, FL

2 sticks butter	1 c. pecans
1 can coconut	4 eggs
2 c. sugar	1 1/2 c. flour

Melt margarine sticks. Put remaining ingredients in mixing bowl and pour melted margarine over all. Mix well. Bake in greased and floured 9 x 13 pan at 350^0 for 40 minutes or until done.

Icing:

7 oz. jar marshmallow cream	1/2 box confectioners sugar
1/4 c. milk	1/3 c. cocoa
3/4 stick margarine	1 tsp. vanilla

Spread marshmallow cream over cake while hot. Mix other ingredients and spread over the cream.

Coconut Cream Cheese Pound Cake
Sandy Skipper, North, SC

1/2 c. soft butter or margarine ·
1/2 c. Crisco
8 oz. cream cheese, softened
3 c. sugar
6 eggs
3 c. plain flour

1 tsp. baking soda
1/4 tsp. salt
6 oz. frozen coconut
1 tsp. vanilla
1 tsp. coconut flavoring

Cream butter, shortening and cream cheese; add sugar and then eggs one at a time. Beat after each addition. Combine flour, soda, and salt and add to creamed ingredients. Stir in other ingredients and bake at 325° about 1 1/2 hours.

Condensed Milk Pound Cake
Sandy Skipper, North, SC

1 lb. butter or margarine
3 c. sugar
1 Tbs. vanilla or lemon flavoring

8 eggs
4 c. plain flour
1 can Eagle Brand condensed milk

Blend butter, sugar and flavorings well. Add eggs 2 at a time, blending well after each addition. Add flour and condensed milk alternately. Blend well and pour into large cake pan. Bake at 300° in a preheated oven about 1 hour and 45 minutes to 2 hours, depending on the oven.

Mexican Fruit Cake
Letha Ray, Salt Rock, WV

1 20 oz. can crushed pineapple,
   undrained
2 c. plain flour
1 tsp. soda

2 c. sugar
2 eggs
1 c. chopped pecans or walnuts

Preheat oven to 350°. Grease 13 x 9 pan with margarine. Mix all ingredients and bake 45 minutes (35 minutes for glass pan). Top with cream cheese frosting.

Red Velvet Pound Cake
Selected

1 1/2 c. shortening (or 1 c. shortening & 1/2 c. margarine)
3 c. sugar   1 c. milk
7 eggs   3 1/2 c. plain flour
2 tsp. vanilla   1/2 tsp. salt
2 oz. red food coloring   1 Tbs. cocoa

Cream shortening and sugar. Add eggs, one at a time and flavoring. Mix food coloring with milk. Combine flour, salt, and cocoa. Add milk and flour mixture alternately to shortening mixture. Blend well at medium speed. Bake at 325⁰ for 1 1/2 to 2 hours.

Red Velvet Cake
Barbara Rogerson, Goose Creek, SC

1/2 c. shortening   1 tsp. baking soda
1 1/2 c. sugar   2 1/2 c. plain flour
2 eggs   1 c. buttermilk
2 oz. red food coloring   2 Tbs. vanilla
1 Tbs. cocoa   1 Tbs. vinegar
1 tsp. salt

Cream shortening and sugar; add eggs. Cream until well blended. Mix food coloring, cocoa and vinegar; add to the creamed mixture. Sift salt, soda and flour. Add dry ingredients and liquids alternately to shortening mixture. Fold, don't beat. Bake in four 9 inch (greased) cake pans at 350⁰ for 30 - 35 minutes.

Pumpkin Crunch
Sonya Greer, Loveland, OH

16 oz. can pumpkin   1 1/2 tsp. cinnamon
12 oz. can evaporated milk 1 box yellow cake mix
3 eggs   1 1/2 stick margarine, melted
1 c. sugar   1 c. chopped nuts (optional)

Combine pumpkin, milk, eggs, sugar and cinnamon; mix well. Pour in 9 x 13 pan. Sprinkle with dry cake mix; drizzle with margarine. Cover with nuts. Bake at 350⁰ 45 - 55 minutes. Serve with Cool Whip.

97

Pumpkin Cake Roll
Selected

Cake:

3 eggs	2 tsp. cinnamon
1 c. sugar	1 tsp. ginger
2/3 c. pumpkin	1/2 tsp. salt
1 tsp. lemon juice	1/2 tsp. nutmeg
3/4 c. flour	1 c. finely chopped pecans
1 tsp. baking powder	

Beat eggs on high speed for 5 minutes; gradually beat in sugar. Stir in pumpkin and lemon juice. Sift together flour, baking powder and spices. Fold in pumpkin. Spread in greased and floured 10 x 15 x 1 inch pan. Top with finely chopped pecans. Bake at 375^0 for 15 minutes. Turn out on towel; sprinkle with powdered sugar. Starting at narrow end, roll towel and cake together; cool. Unroll for filling (below).

Filling:

1 c. powdered sugar	4 Tbs. margarine
2 - 3 oz. pkgs. cream cheese	1/2 tsp. vanilla

Beat until smooth, spread over cake, roll up and chill.

Better Than Anything Cake
Selected

Mix together and layer in bottom of pan:

1 c. graham crackers	1 stick margarine

Mix together and put on first layer:

4 oz. cream cheese	4 oz. Cool Whip
1 c. confectioners sugar	

Mix third layer and put on second layer:
1 small box instant vanilla pudding
1 1/2 c. milk
1 small box strawberry Jell-O (partially setup)

Top with Cool Whip.

Moist Chocolate Cake
Selected

2 c. all purpose flour
1 tsp. salt
1 tsp. baking powder
2 tsp. baking soda
3/4 c. unsweetened cocoa
2 c. sugar

1 c. oil
1 c. hot coffee
1 c. milk
2 eggs
1 tsp. vanilla

Sift together dry ingredients in a mixing bowl. Add oil, coffee and milk. Mix at medium speed for 2 minutes. Add eggs and vanilla; beat 2 more minutes (batter will be thin). Pour into 2 greased and floured 9 in. cake pans. Bake at 325⁰ for 25 - 30 minutes. Cool and add icing.

Banana Split Cake
Kathy De Foor, Godley, TX

Crust:
1 stick margarine
2 c. graham cracker crumbs

Topping:
4 sliced bananas
1 lg. can crushed pineapple, drained

Filling:
2 sticks margarine, softened
2 eggs
1 box powdered sugar
1 tsp. vanilla
1 tsp. butter flavoring

Top with:
1 lg. carton Cool Whip
Pecans, chopped
Maraschino cherries

Melt one stick margarine with 2 cups of graham cracker crumbs. Press into 13 x 9 pan and bake at 350⁰ for 5 minutes. For Filling: Mix filling ingredients and spread over baked crust and chill for 15 minutes. Top with bananas and drained crushed pineapple; then top with Cool Whip, sprinkle with pecans and top with maraschino cherries.

Jell-O Ice Box Cake

Betty Thomas, Greenville, NC

8 oz. pkg. cream cheese, softened	1 c. nuts
1/2 c. powdered sugar	1 box graham crackers
1 lg. container of Cool Whip	2 - 3 oz. pkgs. Jell-O, any flavor
1 lg. can of crushed pineapple, drained	

Mix cream cheese and sugar together; add 1 cup Cool Whip. Mix well, then add pineapple and nuts. Line bottom of long sheet cake pan with graham crackers. Pour the rest of the Cool Whip over top of crackers. Put another layer of crackers over this. Make Jell-O and let it set until it starts to jell. Pour on top of graham crackers. Keep in refrigerator.

Out of This World Cake

Norma Moore, Tyro, NC

2 sticks margarine	1 c. chopped pecans
2 c. sugar	1 c. coconut
4 eggs	1 Tbs. baking powder
1 lb. graham crackers, crushed	1 c. milk

Cream margarine and sugar; add eggs; add crumbs, nuts and coconut. Mix baking powder and add the milk. Bake in three 9 inch greased and floured pans for 40 minutes at 350°.

Frosting:

1 stick margarine, softened	1 Tbs. pineapple juice
1 lg. pkg. cream cheese, softened	1 lg. can crushed pineapple, drained
1 box powdered sugar	

Cream margarine and cream cheese until smooth. Add sugar and pineapple juice. Beat until creamy and top with frosting and drained pineapple.

Quick Fruit Cake

Selected

10 Tbs. butter, cut up
3/4 c. milk
6 Tbs. light corn syrup
2 Tbs. molasses
1 c. currants
3/4 c. pitted dates
3/4 c. golden raisins

1/4 c. chopped mixed candied peel
1 c. walnut pieces
1 3/4 c. all-purpose flour
2 tsp. pumpkin pie spice
1/2 tsp. baking soda
2 eggs

Preheat oven to 300°. In heavy saucepan, combine butter, milk, corn syrup, molasses, currants, dates, raisins, candied peel and walnuts. Heat slowly until butter melts, stirring occasionally. Bring to a simmer over medium heat. Simmer for five minutes, stirring occasionally to prevent sticking. Sift flour, pumpkin pie spice and soda into large bowl. Add fruit mixture and eggs. Whisk until well blended. Line bottom and sides of 8 x 8 x 2 in. pan with double layer of waxed paper. Butter wax paper. Pour batter into pan. Bake for 1 1/2 hours.

Carrot Cake

Alma Schultz, Waycross, GA

2 c. all purpose flour
2 tsp. baking soda
1/2 tsp. salt
1 tsp. cinnamon
3 eggs, beaten
1 1/4 c. oil
1/2 c. buttermilk

2 1/4 c. sugar
2 tsp. vanilla
3 1/2 oz. can of coconut
8 oz. can crushed pineapple, drained
2 c. grated carrots
1 c. chopped walnuts or pecans

Combine flour, soda, salt, cinnamon; set aside. Combine eggs, oil, buttermilk sugar and vanilla. Beat until smooth. Stir in flour mixture, pineapple, carrots, coconut and nuts. Put in 2 greased and floured 9 in. pans. Bake at 350° for 35 to 40 minutes.

Frosting:

8 oz. cream cheese, softened
1/2 c. butter
1 box confectioners sugar (approx.)

1 tsp. vanilla
1 tsp. orange extract

Combine and spread on cooled cake.

Carrot Cake
Velma Smith, Greenville, NC

2 c. all-purpose flour
2 c. sugar
1 1/2 c. oil
4 eggs

2 tsp. cinnamon
1 tsp. salt
1 tsp. baking soda
3 c. grated carrots

Mix dry ingredients, then add oil and eggs. Add carrots last. Bake at 350⁰ for 30 - 40 minutes.

Frosting:
8 oz. cream cheese
1 stick margarine
1 box powdered sugar

1 tsp. vanilla
1 c. chopped walnuts or pecans

Mix and spread on cooled cake.

Carrot Cake
Selected

2 1/2 c. flour
2 c. sugar
1/2 tsp. cinnamon
1 tsp. soda
1 c. oil
1 c. chopped pecans

1 can drained crushed pineapple
1 c. coconut
1 c. raisins
4 eggs
2 c. grated carrots

Mix all ingredients and bake for 1 hour at 300⁰. Frost with Cream Cheese Frosting (above).

Chewies
Shirley Grant, Perry, FL

1 stick of margarine
2 c. brown sugar
2 c. self-rising flour

3 eggs
2 tsp. vanilla
Nuts (opt.)

Mix sugar and butter over low heat until butter is melted, then add flour, eggs, vanilla and nuts. Bake in 9 x 13 pan at 350⁰ for 25 - 30 minutes.

Sock It To Me Cake

Norma Fellure, Hurricane, WV

Cake:

1 pkg. golden cake mix,
  Duncan Hines
1 c. sour cream
1/2 c. oil

1/4 c. sugar
1/4 c. water
4 eggs

Filling:

1 c. chopped pecans
2 Tbs. brown sugar

2 tsp. cinnamon

Preheat oven to 350⁰. In a mixing bowl, blend the cake mix, sour cream, oil, sugar, water and eggs. Beat at high speed for 2 minutes. Pour 2/3 of batter in a greased and floured tube pan. Mix filling and sprinkle over batter. Spread remaining batter over mixture. Bake at 350⁰ for 45 to 55 minutes. Cool right side up. Use confectioners sugar for topping.

Easy Coconut Cake

Norma Moore, Tyro, NC

1 c. flour
1 c. nuts, chopped
1 stick margarine, melted
1 1/2 c. powdered sugar
8 oz. cream cheese, softened

1 c. crushed pineapple
1 lg. carton Cool Whip
2 - 6 oz. pkg. frozen coconut
2 small pkg. instant coconut pudding
3 c. milk

Mix flour, butter and nuts. Press in 9 x 13 pan. Bake at 350⁰ until lightly browned. Let cool. Mix sugar, pineapple, cream cheese; add 1 1/2 cups Cool Whip and 1 package of coconut. Spread on crust. Mix pudding with milk and spread on cake. Spread rest of Cool Whip on cake and top with other package of coconut.

Vanilla Wafer Cake
Selected

1 c. butter	1 tsp. vanilla
2 c. sugar	1 c. chopped nuts
6 eggs	1 c. coconut
1/2 c. milk	12 oz. box vanilla wafers, crushed

Cream butter and sugar. Add eggs one at a time, beat well. Add milk and vanilla; mix well. Add pecans, coconut and vanilla wafers; mix well. Pour into a greased and floured tube pan. Bake at 350° for 1 hour.

Angel Food Cake
Selected

1 doz. jumbo egg whites	1 3/4 c. sugar (divided)
1/2 tsp. salt	1 tsp. vanilla
1 1/2 tsp. cream of tartar	1 c. flour

Beat egg whites until stiff. Add salt and cream of tartar and beat until peaks are formed. Then gradually add 3/4 cup of sugar. Beat with wire whisk. Add vanilla. In another bowl, mix flour and 1 c. sugar together. Gradually add the egg white mixture to the flour mixture. Pour into an angel food cake pan. Bake for 35 minutes in a 350° oven.

Honey Bun Cake
Norma Moore, Tyro, NC

1 box yellow cake mix	Mix together for swirl:
1 c. oil	3/4 c. brown sugar
4 eggs	4 tsp. cinnamon
4 Tbs. sugar	
1 c. buttermilk	

Mix cake ingredients and reserve 1 c. of batter. Take the 1 c. of batter and add swirl ingredients. Swirl with edge of knife into cake. Be sure to cover swirl with cake batter. Bake at 325° for 40 minutes or until cake is golden brown.

Fudge Filled Cupcakes

Sonya Greer, Loveland, OH

2/3 c. chocolate chips	4 large eggs
1 1/4 tsp. vanilla	1 1/2 c. sugar
6 oz. margarine	1 c. all purpose flour

Filling:

1 8 oz. pkg. cream cheese	1 lg. egg
1/4 c. sugar	1/2 c. chocolate chips

Preheat oven to 350⁰. Melt together 2/3 c. chocolate chips, vanilla and margarine in double boiler. Beat eggs till frothy; gradually beat in sugar till it dissolves. Gradually beat in flour. Fold in chocolate mixture. Mix together cream cheese, sugar and eggs till blended. Fold in 1/2 c. chocolate chips. Drop teaspoonful of filling into cupcake tins; cover with chocolate mixture. Bake for 25 - 30 minutes.

One, Two, Three, Four Cake

Ruby Pickens, Canton, NC

1 c. butter or shortening	3 c. sifted cake flour
2 c. sugar	1/4 tsp. salt
4 eggs, separated	3 tsp. baking powder
1 tsp. vanilla	1 c. powdered milk

Cream shortening and sugar until fluffy. Add egg yolks one at a time, beating thoroughly after each one. Sift dry ingredients together 3 times and add alternately with milk and vanilla to creamed mixture, beating until smooth after each addition. Fold in stiffly beaten egg whites. Pour into greased and floured pans. Bake at 350⁰ for 25 minutes. Makes 3 (9 inch) layers.

COOKIES
Chewy Chocolate Macaroons

Vicki Richburg, Six Mile, SC

1 pkg. (14 oz.) coconut	4 squares unsweetened chocolate,
1 can sweetened condensed milk	melted
2 tsp. vanilla	

Combine all ingredients in a bowl and mix well. Drop from teaspoon, 1 inch apart on well-greased baking sheet. Bake at 350⁰ for 10 to 12 minutes. Remove from baking sheet at once.

Butterscotch Grahams

Betty Thomas, Greenville, NC

1 c. butter (2 sticks)	1 c. chopped walnuts
1 c. brown sugar, packed	24 graham crackers

Combine butter and sugar; place over heat. Bring to boil and boil three minutes. Stir in nuts. Line a 15 x 10 baking pan with graham crackers. Spread mixture over crackers. Bake 10 minutes in 325⁰ oven. Cut into bars while warm.

Neiman Marcus Cookies

Chris Perrine, Milton, FL

2 c. butter	1 tsp. salt
2 c. sugar	2 tsp. baking powder
2 c. brown sugar	2 tsp. baking soda
4 eggs	24 oz. chocolate chips
2 tsp. vanilla	8 oz. Hershey bar, chopped
4 c. flour	3 c. chopped nuts
5 c. oatmeal, blended in blender	

Cream butter and sugars; add eggs and vanilla. Mix together with flour, oatmeal, salt, baking powder, and soda. Add chocolate chips, Hershey bar and chopped nuts. (I chop mine in the blender.) Roll into balls and place 2 inches apart on cookie sheet. Bake at 375⁰ for 10 minutes. Makes 112 cookies.

Note: You can cut this recipe in half.

No Bake Cookies

Jennifer Fellure, Milton, FL

2 c. sugar	1 tsp. vanilla
1/2 c. cocoa	3/4 c. peanut butter
1/2 c. milk	2 c. minute oats
1/4 c. butter	

Bring sugar, cocoa, milk, butter and vanilla to boil. Remove from heat and add peanut butter and oats. Mix well and drop onto wax paper . Let cool until cookies are set.

Lemon Bars

Kathy DeFoor, Godley, TX

1 box lemon cake mix	8 oz. cream cheese, softened
1/2 c. butter, melted	2 eggs
1 egg	2 1/2 c. powdered sugar

Mix cake mix, butter and egg and pat into greased 9 x 13 pan. Mix cream cheese, eggs and powdered sugar and pour on top. Bake at 350^0 for 35 to 40 minutes or until golden brown. Note: You may use other flavors of cake mix.

Outrageous Chocolate Chip Cookies

Barbara Rogerson, Goose Creek, SC

1/2 c. sugar	1 egg
1/3 c. brown sugar	1 c. self rising flour
1/2 c. margarine	1/2 c. quick oatmeal
1/2 c. peanut butter	1 pkg. (6 oz.) semisweet chocolate
1/2 tsp. vanilla	chips

Heat oven to 350^0. Beat sugars, margarine, peanut butter, vanilla and egg in medium size bowl with wooden spoon until creamy and well blended. Mix in flour and oatmeal. Stir in chocolate chips. Drop by rounded tablespoonfuls about 2 inches apart on ungreased cookie sheet. Bake 8 to 10 minutes.

Black Bottom Banana Bars
Selected

1/2 c. margarine, softened	1 1/2 c. all-purpose flour
1 c. sugar	1 tsp. baking powder
1 egg	1 tsp. baking soda
1 tsp. vanilla	1/2 tsp. salt
1 1/2 c. mashed bananas	1/4 c. baking cocoa

In a mixing bowl, cream butter and sugar. Add egg and vanilla, beating until thoroughly combined. Blend in bananas. Combine the flour, baking powder, baking soda and salt; add to creamed mixture and mix well. Divide batter in half. Add cocoa to half. Spread into a greased 13 x 9 x 2 baking pan. Spoon remaining batter on top and swirl with knife. Bake at 350⁰ for 25 minutes or until bars test done.

Mom's Soft Raisin Cookies
Selected

1 c. water	1 tsp. baking powder
2 c. raisins	1 tsp. baking soda
1 c. shortening	1 tsp. salt
1 3/4 c. sugar	1/2 tsp. ground cinnamon
2 eggs, slightly beaten	1/2 tsp. ground nutmeg
1 tsp. vanilla	1/2 tsp. chopped walnuts
3 1/2 c. all-purpose flour	

Combine raisins and water in a small saucepan; bring to a boil. Cook for 3 minutes. Remove from heat and let cool (do not drain). In a mixing bowl, cream shortening; gradually add sugar. Add eggs and vanilla. Combine dry ingredients; gradually add to creamed mixture and blend thoroughly. Stir in nuts and raisins. Drop by teaspoon 2 inches apart on greased baking sheet. Bake at 350⁰ for 12 minutes.

Oreo Cookie Dessert

Jennifer Fellure, Milton, FL

1 bag Oreos
2 small instant vanilla pudding
3 c. milk

1 1/2 c. powdered sugar
13 oz. Cool Whip
8 oz. sour cream

Use half of the crumbled cookies and place in a 9 x 13 pan. Mix pudding and milk until done, add other ingredients and pour over cookies. Top with remaining cookies.

Scotch-A-Roos

Lisa Bailes, Summersville, WV

1 c. sugar
1 c. white syrup
1 c. peanut butter

5 c. Rice Krispies
6 oz. pkg. chocolate chips
6 oz. pkg. butterscotch chips

Mix sugar and syrup in sauce pan and cook until it bubbles. Add peanut butter; mix well. Add Rice Krispies and mix. Pour in a buttered 9 x 13 pan and press down with your hands. Melt both kinds of chips in double broiler and spread over Krispy mixture.

Date Nut Balls

Barbara Rogerson, Goose Creek, SC

1 c. chopped dates
1 c. sugar
1 egg, well beaten
1 stick margarine

1 c. chopped nuts
1 tsp. vanilla
2 c. Rice Krispies
Confectioners sugar or coconut

Combine all ingredients, except Rice Krispies, vanilla, and confectioners sugar. Cook for 10 minutes, stirring constantly. Remove from heat and add Rice Krispies and vanilla. Set aside to cool. When cooled enough to handle, form into balls and roll in confectioners sugar or coconut. Note: Have to work fast because they get too hard to roll.

Peanut Butter - Chocolate Kisses

Heidi Berg, Milton, FL

1/2 c. sugar	1 1/2 c. whole wheat flour
1/2 c. brown sugar	3/4 tsp. baking soda
1/2 c. peanut butter	1/2 tsp. baking powder
1/4 c. margarine, softened	Extra sugar
1/4 c. shortening	3 doz. chocolate kisses
1 egg	

Mix sugar, brown sugar, peanut butter, margarine, shortening and egg in a large bowl; stir in wheat flour, soda, and baking powder. Shape dough into 1" balls; roll in sugar. Place 2" a part on ungreased cookie sheet. Bake 8 -10 minutes at 375^0. Immediately, press candy kiss in each cookie. Cool and eat.

Gingersnaps

Elsie Gilkerson, Milton, FL

1 c. molasses	1 Tbs. baking soda
1 c. sugar	2 Tbs. ginger
1 c. shortening	4 c. sifted flour
2 eggs	

Mix ingredients in the order given to make a stiff dough. Roll into marble-sized balls. Bake in moderate oven (350^0) until brown. Makes about 4 dozen.

Lemon Sugar Cookies

Lanee Osborn, New Caney, TX

1 c. powdered sugar	1 1/2 - 2 tsp. lemon flavor
1 c. sugar	1 tsp. cream of tartar
2 sticks butter	1 tsp. soda
2 eggs	1 tsp. salt
1 c. oil	5 c. flour
2 tsp. vanilla	

Mix all ingredients well. Bake at 350^0 until edges of cookies are brown. Don't overbake.

German Chocolate Chess Squares

Dorothy Grady, Mt.Olive, NC

1 box German chocolate cake mix
  (with pudding)
1 lg. egg, slightly beaten
1/2 c. butter or margarine
1 c. chopped pecans

8 oz. cream cheese, softened
2 lg. eggs
16 oz. box powdered sugar

Combine first four ingredients in bowl stirring until dry ingredients are moistened. Press into bottom of greased 13 x 9 pan. Combine cream cheese, 2 eggs and 1 cup powdered sugar; beat at medium speed with electric mixer until blended. Gradually add remaining powdered sugar, beating after each addition. Pour over chocolate layer spreading evenly. Bake at 350° for 40 minutes. Cool on rack and cut in squares.

Quick Easy Brownies

Maddy Ray, Tempe, AZ

1 stick oleo, melted
6 Tbs. cocoa
2 c. sugar
4 or 5 eggs

1 tsp. vanilla
2 c. flour
Dash of salt
1 c. nuts

Mix together and spread on greased cookie sheet with an edge (17 x 10). Bake 17 minutes at 350°.

Brownies

Vicki Richburg, Six Mile, SC

2 1 oz. squares unsweetened
  chocolate
1/2 c. shortening
3/4 c. flour
1/2 tsp. baking powder

1/2 tsp. salt
2 eggs
1 c. sugar
1 tsp. vanilla
1 c. walnuts

Melt shortening and chocolate together over hot water; cool. Sift together flour, baking powder and salt. Beat eggs until light; stir in sugar; then blend in chocolate mixture, vanilla & nuts. Bake at 350° for 30 - 35 min.

Peanut Butter Cookies

Kate Cravatt, Brewton, AL

1/2 c. shortening
1/3 c. peanut butter
1 c. sugar
1 egg (well beaten)

1/2 tsp. salt
1 1/2 c. cake flour
1 tsp. soda
1/2 tsp. vanilla

Cream shortening, peanut butter and sugar together. Add egg. Sift dry ingredients together and add to first mixture. Add vanilla and mix well. Form into small balls and place on cookie sheet. Flatten with fork and bake at 350⁰ for 12 minutes.

Oatmeal Cookies

Chris Perrine, Milton, FL

1/4 c. shortening
1 c. sugar
2 eggs
1 c. plus 2 Tbs. flour
1 tsp. baking powder
1/4 tsp. salt

1/3 c. milk
1 tsp. cinnamon
1 tsp. vanilla
3 c. oatmeal
1 c. seedless raisins, optional

Mix all ingredients thoroughly. Drop by teaspoonfuls onto a greased cookie sheet and bake at 375⁰ for 15 minutes. Makes 4 dozen.

Applesauce Cookies

Elsie Gilkerson, Milton, FL

1 c. sugar (either white or brown)
1/2 c. shortening
1 1/2 c. unsweetened applesauce
2 tsp. baking soda
2 1/4 c. flour

1/2 tsp. ground cloves
1 tsp. cinnamon
1/2 tsp. salt
1 c. raisins
1/2 c. nuts

Cream together sugar and shortening. Add applesauce in which the soda has been dissolved. Sift the flour, spices and salt; add raisins and nuts and drop several inches apart onto a greased baking sheet. Bake slowly (300⁰) about 15 minutes. Makes 30 cookies.

Mounds Bars
Vickie Baker, Loveland, OH

1 pkg. graham crackers, crushed
  (app. 11 whole crackers)
1/3 c. butter or margarine
1 can sweetened condensed milk

2 c. flaked coconut
12 oz. semisweet chocolate chips,
  melted

Preheat oven to 350⁰. Mix graham cracker crumbs and butter and pat in bottom of 9 x 13 pan. Bake for 5 to 8 minutes. Mix sweetened condensed milk and coconut. Spread on crust. Bake 15 more minutes. When cool, cover with melted chocolate chips. Cool and cut into cookie size bars.

Peanut Butter Crispy Treats
Vicki Richburg, Six Mile, SC

1 c. light or dark corn syrup
1 c. sugar

1 c. peanut butter
6 c. Rice Krispies cereal

Grease 13 x 9 inch baking pan. In large saucepan stir together corn syrup, sugar and peanut butter over low heat. Stirring constantly, bring to a boil. Remove from heat. Add cereal, tossing to coat well. Press into prepared pan. Cool.

The World's Best Cookies
Barbara Rogerson, Goose Creek, SC

1 c. butter, softened
1 c. sugar
1 c. brown sugar
1 egg
1 c. oil
1 c. crushed cornflakes
1 c. oatmeal

1/2 c. chopped nuts
1/2 c. coconut
3 1/2 c. sifted flour
1 tsp. soda
1 tsp. salt
1 tsp. vanilla

Cream butter and sugars until fluffy; add egg & oil and mix well. Add oatmeal, cornflakes, coconut, nuts and stir well. Sift dry ingredients; add to butter mixture. Mix well and add vanilla. Drop by teaspoonfuls on ungreased cookie sheet or make into small balls. Bake at 325⁰ for 12 minutes.

Peanut Butter Cornflakes

Barbara Rogerson, Goose Creek, SC

1 c. sugar
1 c. Karo syrup

1 c. peanut butter
6 c. cornflakes

Mix sugar, syrup and peanut butter; cook in microwave 3 minutes, 10 seconds. Take out and add cornflakes, mixing and stirring until cornflakes are coated. Spoon onto wax paper and let cool.

Snickerdoodles

Selected

1/2 c. shortening
1/2 c. butter, softened
1 1/2 c. sugar
2 eggs
2 3/4 c. all-purpose flour

2 tsp. cream of tartar
1/4 tsp. salt
1 tsp. soda
2 Tbs. sugar
2 Tbs. cinnamon

Mix thoroughly shortening, butter, sugar and eggs. Blend in the flour, cream of tartar, soda and salt. Cover and chill. Mix the sugar and cinnamon. Roll balls in mixture and bake on ungreased cookie sheet 8 to 10 minutes at 350⁰.

Pumpkin Chocolate Chip Cookies

Selected

1 c. butter or margarine, softened
3/4 c. brown sugar
3/4 c. sugar
1 egg
1 tsp. vanilla extract
2 c. all-purpose flour

1 c. quick cooking oats
1 tsp. baking soda
1 tsp. ground cinnamon
1 c. cooked or canned pumpkin
1 1/2 c. semisweet chocolate chips

In a mixing bowl, cream butter and sugars. Beat in egg and vanilla. Combine flour, oats, baking soda and cinnamon; stir into creamed mixture alternately with pumpkin. Fold in chocolate chips. Drop by tablespoonfuls onto greased baking sheet. Bake at 350⁰ for 12 - 13 minutes or until lightly browned. Yields about 4 dozen.

Peanut Butter Chocolate Chip Cookies
Selected

1 c. butter	1 tsp. baking soda
1 1/2 c. sugar	1/2 tsp. salt
2 eggs	12 oz. Reese's peanut butter chips
2 tsp. vanilla	12 oz. pkg. chocolate chips
2 c. flour	2 c. pecans, chopped
2/3 c. cocoa	

Cream butter, sugar, eggs, and vanilla until fluffy in a large mixer bowl. Combine flour, cocoa, soda and salt; blend into creamed mixture. Stir in peanut butter chips, chocolate chips and nuts. Drop by rounded teaspoonfuls onto a greased cookie sheet. Bake at 350⁰ for 8 to 10 minutes. Makes 5 dozen.

Peanut Butter Cups
Selected

1 1/3 c. graham cracker crumbs	1 c. peanut butter
2 sticks margarine (softened)	1 box powdered sugar

Mix ingredients well and pat into a 9 x 13 baking pan.

Topping:

1/2 c. peanut butter	12 oz. chocolate chips

Melt and pour over the above. Let cool and cut as desired.

Pecan Sandies
Selected

2 sticks margarine	1/2 tsp. vanilla
1 3/4 c. all purpose flour	1/2 c. chopped pecans
1/2 c. sifted powdered sugar	Powdered sugar to coat

Mix thoroughly and chill. Shape into one inch balls on cookie sheet. Bake for 20 minutes at 350⁰. Cool and shake in powdered sugar.

Applesauce Raisin Bars
Vicki Richburg, Six Mile, SC

2 c. applesauce	1 1/2 c. unbleached flour
3/4 c. margarine	1 c. whole wheat flour
1 c. brown sugar	1 tsp. baking soda
1 tsp. cinnamon	1/2 tsp. salt
1/4 tsp. cloves	1 egg, slightly beaten
1 1/2 c. raisins	1 c. walnuts, chopped

In a saucepan, heat together applesauce, butter, sugar, cinnamon, cloves and raisins, but do not boil; allow to cool. Mix flours, soda and salt and stir into applesauce mixture with egg and nuts. Spread in a greased 10 x 15 inch baking sheet with a lip and bake at 350⁰ for 30 minutes.

Sugar Cookies
Selected

1 1/2 c. powdered sugar	1 tsp. almond extract
1 c. butter	2 1/2 c. flour
1 egg	1 tsp. soda
1 tsp. vanilla extract	1 tsp. cream of tarter

Mix sugar, butter, egg, and flavorings; add dry ingredients. Bake at 350⁰ for 8 to 10 minutes.

Christmas Sugar Cookies
Selected

3/4 c. sugar	1 1/2 c. flour
1/2 c. margarine, softened	1 tsp. baking powder
1 egg	1/4 tsp. salt
1/2 tsp. vanilla	

Cream together sugar and margarine. Add egg and vanilla. Beat until fluffy. Sift together flour, baking powder and salt. Stir dry ingredients, gradually into sugar-margarine mixture. Refrigerate overnight. Roll out dough to 1/4 inch thick. Cut into shapes and place on an ungreased cookie sheet. Decorate with colored sugar. Bake for 8 to 10 minutes at 375⁰.

Ice Box Pecan Cookies
Faye Chapman, Milton, WV

1/2 lb. butter	1/2 tsp. baking powder
1 c. brown sugar	1/2 tsp. baking soda
1 c. white sugar	1 tsp. vanilla extract
1 egg	1 c. chopped pecans
3 c. flour	

Mix butter, sugars and egg together in a bowl. Add flour, baking powder and soda. Add vanilla and chopped nuts. Roll in waxed paper and chill until hard. Slice very thin and place on a greased baking pan. Bake at 350° until golden brown.

Frozen Chocolate Torte
Selected

1 pkg. (10 1/2 oz.) miniature marshmallows	1 c. flaked coconut
	1/2 c. margarine
1 c. semisweet chocolate chips	2 c. graham cracker crumbs
1 can evaporated milk (12 oz.)	1/2 gal. vanilla ice cream, softened

In a saucepan over low heat, melt marshmallows and chocolate chips with evaporated milk. Remove from heat. Cool. In a skillet, stir coconut in butter until browned. Remove from the heat; stir in crumbs. Pat three-fourths into a 9 x 13 baking pan; cool. Spoon half of the ice cream onto crust. Top with half of the chocolate mixture. Layer with remaining ice cream and chocolate. Sprinkle with remaining crumbs. Cover and freeze for 2 hours.

117

Molasses Cookies

Madeline Darnell, Sulphur, LA

1/2 c. shortening, softened	1 tsp. soda
1 c. sugar	1 1/2 tsp. salt
1 egg	1 1/2 tsp. ginger
1 c. dark molasses	1/2 tsp. cloves
1/2 c. water	1/4 tsp. allspice
4 c. sifted flour	

Mix well shortening, sugar and egg. Stir in molasses and water. Sift together flour, soda, salt, ginger, cloves, and allspice. Chill dough several hours or overnight. Roll out 1/4 in. thick and cut in shapes. Place on well greased baking sheet. Bake 10 to 12 minutes at 375⁰. Leave on cookie sheet to cool slightly before removing to prevent breaking.

PIES
Three Minute Yogurt Pie

Selected

2 (8 oz.) cartons lemon yogurt	9 oz. whipped topping
1 Tbs. grated lemon rind	1 (9 in.) graham cracker crust

Blend yogurt and lemon rind into whipped topping. Pour into pie shell. Freeze about four hours or until firm. Remove from freezer 30 minutes before serving.

Key Lime Pie

Selected

4 egg yolks	6 oz. Cool Whip
(save whites for meringue)	4 Tbs. powdered sugar
1 can sweetened condensed milk	Pie shell, regular or graham
1/2 c. key lime juice	

Beat egg yolks. Stir in condensed milk, then add key lime juice slowly. Then add Cool Whip, stirring gently. The mixture will thicken. Pour into cooled baked pie shell or graham cracker crust. Make meringue of the 4 egg whites, beating in 4 tablespoons powdered sugar. Sprinkle a little grated lime rind on top. Brown meringue. Refrigerate overnight.

Million Dollar Pie

Betty Thomas, Greenville, NC

1 can Eagle Brand milk
1/4 c. lemon juice
1 c. chopped pecans
1 lg. can crushed pineapple, drained

1 lg. Cool Whip
2 pie shells, baked & cooled

Mix milk and lemon juice together; add nuts and pineapple and mix well. Lightly fold Cool Whip into mixture. Pour into graham cracker crusts or baked & cooled pie shells. Chill before cutting.

Pecan Pie

Shelby Perry, Lexington, NC

5 eggs
1 1/2 c. sugar
3/4 c. Karo syrup

6 Tbs. melted margarine
1 1/2 c. finely chopped pecans

Mix all ingredients and bake at 375⁰ for 35 minutes. Cover with Bake Saran Wrap shortly after taking out of the oven.

Baked Chocolate Pecan Pie

Betty Thomas, Greenville, NC

1 1/2 c. sugar
3 1/2 Tbs. cocoa
1 small can evaporated milk
2 eggs

1/2 stick margarine, melted
1 tsp. vanilla
1/2 c. pecans

Mix sugar and cocoa; add other ingredients and mix well. Pour into unbaked pie shell. Bake at 350⁰ for 45 minutes.

Cinnamon Pecan Pie

Selected

1 stick margarine, softened
1 lb. light brown sugar
1 small can condensed milk
4 eggs

1 tsp. vanilla
1 1/2 tsp. cinnamon
1 c. chopped pecans

Mix margarine, sugar and milk; let set overnight. Beat eggs; add to mix. Add vanilla, cinnamon and nuts. Bake at 350⁰ for 30 to 40 minutes, until slightly firm. Makes 2 pies.

New Pecan Pie

Norma Moore, Tyro, NC

1 stick margarine, softened
1 box lt. brown sugar
4 eggs, beaten
4 Tbs. milk

2 tsp. lt. corn syrup
1 tsp. vanilla
2 c. chopped pecans

Mix all ingredients. Bake at 350⁰ for 30 minutes or until done in the middle. Makes two pies.

Coconut Pie

Barbara Rogerson, Goose Creek, SC

1/2 c. margarine, softened
1 1/2 c. sugar
1 c. milk
4 eggs

1/2 c. self-rising flour
1 1/4 c. coconut
1 Tbs. vanilla

Mix all ingredients and pour into 2 greased pie pans or 2 unbaked pie shells. Bake at 350⁰ for 30 - 40 minutes. Let pies remain in oven 10 minutes more.

Coconut Pie

Selected

1 1/2 c. milk	3 Tbs. all-purpose flour
1 c. sugar	1 Tbs. margarine, melted
3/4 c. coconut	1/4 tsp. vanilla
2 eggs, beaten	1 unbaked pie shell

In large bowl, mix all ingredients until well blended. Pour into pie shell. Bake at 350⁰ for 50 minutes or until knife inserted in center comes out clean. Cool and refrigerate.

Fluffy Peanut Butter Pie

Maddy Ray, Tempe, AZ

1/2 c. peanut butter, creamy or crunchy	1/2 c. milk
8 oz. cream cheese, softened	9 oz. Cool Whip, thawed
1 c. powdered sugar	1/4 c. peanuts, finely chopped
	9 in. graham cracker crumb crust

Whip cheese until soft and fluffy. Beat in peanut butter and sugar. Slowly add milk, blending thoroughly into mixture. Fold Cool Whip into mixture. Pour into 9 in. graham cracker crumb crust. Sprinkle with chopped peanuts. Freeze until firm.

Betty's Pie Crust

Betty DeJarnett, Orando, WA

3 c. flour	1 egg
1 1/2 c. shortening	2 tsp. vinegar

Cut shortening into flour. Beat egg and vinegar and add enough water to make 2/3 cup. Mix together and roll out. Makes three crusts.

Chocolate Pie

Julie Waller, New Caney, TX

2/3 c. sugar
3 Tbs. cocoa
2 eggs
1 tsp. vanilla

3 Tbs. flour
Dash of salt
2 c. Pet milk
1 stick margarine

Combine all ingredients, except margarine. Cook on medium heat until thickens. Remove from heat, add margarine. Stir till blended well. Pour into baked pie shell. Put in refrigerator until very cold. Top whole pie with Cool Whip.

Southern Chocolate Pie

Norma Moore, Tyro, NC

1 1/2 c. sugar
1/2 c. cocoa
1/4 c. flour
3 egg yolks

2 c. milk
1 tsp. vanilla
Pinch of salt

Combine ingredients and cook until thick. Pour into baked shell and add meringue. Makes 2 small pies or 1 large.

German Chocolate Pie

Norma Moore, Tyro, NC

6 Tbs. cocoa
4 eggs
3 c. sugar
1 lg. can evaporated milk

6 tsp. vanilla
1 stick margarine, melted
1 c. pecans, chopped
2 c. coconut

Mix well. Pour into 3 unbaked pie shells. Bake at 350^0 for 35 minutes or until pie doesn't shake in middle.

Quick Chocolate Pie
Dorothy Grady, Mt. Olive, NC

4 oz. pkg. chocolate pudding
  & pie filling (cooked kind)
1/4 c. sugar

2 egg yolks
2 c. milk
2 Tbs. butter

Mix pudding, sugar, egg yolks & milk. Cook in microwave until thickened, about 5 minutes. Stir at least once during the five minutes. Add butter and return to microwave for three more minutes. Pour in baked pie shell and top with meringue.

Peanut Butter Pie
Faye Chapman, Milton, WV

9 oz. graham cracker crust
1 c. peanut butter
1 1/2 c. confectioners sugar

1 lg. French vanilla instant pudding
Cool Whip
Nuts on top (optional)

Mix peanut butter and sugar slowly and put into crust. Mix pudding according to directions and pour over peanut butter mixture. Spread Cool Whip on top of pudding. Top with nuts.

Mock Apple Pie
Martha Mericle, Groveton, TX

Unbaked pie shell (2 crust)
Tube of Ritz crackers, broken
2 Tbs. butter

Cinnamon
Nutmeg

Bring to boil:
1 1/2 c. water
1 1/2 c. sugar

1 Tbs. butter
2 tsp. cream of tartar.

Sprinkle crackers with cinnamon and a dash of nutmeg. Dot with butter. Pour boiling mixture over crackers. Cover with top crust; sprinkle sugar/ cinnamon on crust. Poke fork holes in top crust and bake for approximately 30 minutes at 375^0.

Apple Crisp

Donna Lisenbee, Boaz, FL

1 can (22 oz.) apple filling
1 c. quick oatmeal
1/2 c. butter, softened
1/2 c. brown sugar, packed

1/4 c. flour
1 tsp. cinnamon
1/2 tsp. nutmeg

Spread apple pie filling in a 1 1/2 qt. baking dish. Combine other ingredients and spread over filling. Bake at 325° for 25 - 35 minutes.

Easy Apple Pie

Betty Thomas, Greenville, NC

1/2 stick melted butter
1 c. sugar
1 egg
1 tsp. vanilla

1 c. self-rising flour
1 tsp. cinnamon
1/4 tsp. nutmeg
1 1/2 c. chopped apples

Mix all ingredients in a large bowl in order given. Bake in pie pan at 350° for one hour.

Fresh Apple Pie

Mary Fellure, Milton, FL

1 1/2 c. sugar
3 Tbs. flour
1/2 c. margarine, melted
1/2 tsp. nutmeg

1/2 tsp. cinnamon
1 tsp. vanilla
3 c. sliced apples, cooked tender

Mix ingredients and pour into unbaked pie shell. Place top crust on pie and bake at 300° for 20 minutes. Turn to 325° for about 20 more minutes if needed until golden brown.

Lazy Magic Pumpkin Pie

Selected

3/4 c. sugar	3 eggs
4 Tbs. oleo	16 oz. can of pumpkin
1/2 c. self-rising flour	3 tsp. pumpkin pie spice
1 lg. can evaporated milk	2 tsp. vanilla flavoring

Heat oven to 350⁰. Lightly grease a 10-inch pie plate. On high speed in blender, beat ingredients 1 minute or 2 minutes with hand beater. Bake until golden brown and knife inserted in center comes out clean, approx. 50 - 55 minutes. This makes its own crust.

Double Layer Pumpkin Pie

Selected

4 oz. cream cheese, softened	1 1/2 c. thawed Cool Whip
1 Tbs. milk	1 graham cracker crust
1 Tbs. sugar	

Mix cream cheese, milk and sugar in large bowl until smooth (with wire whisk). Gently stir in Cool Whip. Spread on graham cracker crust.

2 pkgs. vanilla instant pudding	1/2 tsp. ginger
1 c. cold milk	1/4 tsp. cloves
16 oz. can pumpkin	1 tsp. cinnamon

Pour 1 cup milk in bowl; add pudding mixes. Beat with wire whisk about one minute, mixture will be thick. Stir in pumpkin and spices with whisk until well mixed. Spread over cream cheese mixture. Refrigerate for four hours or until set.

Pumpkin Pie

Mary Jackson, Lexington, NC

1 c. brown sugar	1 2/3 c. evaporated milk
2 c. pumpkin	1 Tbs. flour
1/2 tsp. salt	2 tsp. pumpkin pie spice
1 egg	1/2 tsp. butter flavoring

Mix well; pour into deep dish shell. Bake at 325⁰ for 40 minutes.

Pecan Pie

Chris Perrine, Milton, FL

9 in. unbaked pie shell	1/4 tsp. salt
1/2 c. margarine	1 tsp. vanilla
1c. sugar	1 1/2 c. chopped pecans
3 eggs (slightly beaten)	Whole pecan meats
3/4 c. dark corn syrup	

Chill pie shell thoroughly. Set oven for moderate tempature (375^0). Cream margarine; add sugar gradually and continue beating until light and fluffy. Add eggs, syrup, salt, vanilla and chopped pecans. Pour into pie shell. Bake 40 to 45 minutes. Garnish with whole nuts.

Easy Pie Cobbler

Chris Perrine, Milton, FL

1/2 stick margarine	1 c. milk
1 c. flour	Fruit of your choice
1 c. sugar	

Melt margarine in bottom of pan. Mix flour, sugar and milk and pour into melted margarine. Add favorite fruit to top and bake at 350^0 for 35 - 40 minutes or until golden brown.

Easy Pie Cobbler

Elsie Gilkerson, Milton, FL

Stick of butter or margarine	1 c. buttermilk
1 c. flour	Pinch of soda
1 c. sugar	Berries and juice, app. 3 c.

Melt butter in 9 x 13 pan. Combine flour, sugar, milk and soda. Pour over butter and add favorite berries and juice. Bake at 350^0 for 45 minutes or until golden brown.

Easy Pie Cobbler

Susan Taylor, Brunswick, GA

1 c. self-rising flour	1/2 stick margarine
1 c. sugar	1 or 2 cans of fruit, drained
1 c. milk	

Melt butter in 13 x 9 pan. Mix flour, sugar, and milk and pour half of mixture in buttered pan. Pour in fruit and then cover with remaining flour mixture. Bake at 350^0 for 45 minutes to 1 hour.

Chess Pie

Lillian Miller, Murfreesboro, TN

1 Tbs. flour	1 tsp. vanilla
1 Tbs. cornmeal	3 whole eggs
1 1/2 c. sugar	4 Tbs. milk
1 Tbs. vinegar	1 stick of margarine (melted)

Combine all ingredients and bake at 350^0 for 45 minutes.

Sweet Potato Pie

Gladys Coker, New Caney, TX

2 c. cooked (mashed sweet potatoes)	
1/2 c. butter	1/2 tsp. nutmeg
2 egg yolks	1/2 tsp. ginger
1 c. brown sugar	1/2 c. milk
1/4 tsp. salt	5 egg whites (beat with 1/4 c. sugar
1/2 tsp. cinnamon	until stiff)

Mix the first eight ingredients with warm potatoes; add milk. Fold in egg white mixture. Put in pie shell. Bake at 400^0 for 10 minutes, then lower temp. to 350^0. Bake until set.

Buttermilk Pie

Georgia Prentice, Temple, AZ

4 eggs
1 1/2 c. sugar
1 c. buttermilk
3 Tbs. flour

Pinch of salt
1/2 tsp. nutmeg
1/2 tsp. all spice
1/2 c. butter

Mix all together. Bake in uncooked pie shell for 45 min. at 325°.

Impossible Pie

Chris Perrine, Milton, FL

1 c. sugar
2 c. milk
1/2 c. flour
1 c. coconut

1 stick of margarine
2 tsp. vanilla
4 eggs
1/2 tsp. salt

Mix all the ingredients, except coconut into blender (or mixer). Mix until smooth. Then add coconut and mix with spoon. Pour into 9" pie pan;bake at 350° for 40 to 45 minutes.
Note: This pie makes its own crust.

Fruit Cocktail Pie

Faye Chapman, Milton, WV

1 lb. can fruit cocktail
3 oz. lemon Jell-O gelatin
1/2 c. cold water

Pint of vanilla ice cream
Vanilla wafers

Drain fruit cocktail; save juice and add water to make 1 cup liquid. Heat juice to boiling, add gelatin and dissolve; add the cold water. Cut ice cream into 6 slices; add to Jell-O mixture. Stir until melted. Chill until thickened, 15 to 20 minutes. Fold in fruit cocktail. Layer in 9 in. pie pan with vanilla wafers, bottom and side. Pour filling into pan and let set for 45 minutes or more.

Peach Pie
Geraldine Chapman, Brunswick, GA

4 c. thinly sliced fresh peaches
3/4 c. sugar
3 Tbs. quick tapioca

1/4 tsp. salt
2 Tbs. margarine
2 pie shells

Combine first four ingredients; turn into pie shell. Dot with margarine. Cover with second pie shell. Bake at 425⁰ for 40 minutes.

Old Fashioned Sweet Potato Pudding
Betty Thomas, Greenville, NC

4 1/2 c. of mashed sweet potatoes
3 c. sugar
1 c. milk

3 lg. eggs
1 Tbs. ground allspice or cloves
1 3/4 stick margarine, melted

Mix all ingredients thoroughly. Pour into large greased pan. Preheat oven to 375⁰ and bake for 30 minutes.

Three Layer Pie
Barbara Rogerson, Goose Creek, SC

Crust:
1 c. self-rising flour
1 c. chopped nuts

1 stick margarine

Filling:
1 c. powdered sugar
1 - 8 oz. cream cheese

1 c. Cool Whip

Pudding:
1 lg. pkg. instant chocolate pudding

Melt margarine; add flour and nuts. Mix and press into a baking dish. Bake at 350⁰ for 25 to 30 minutes. Let cool completely. Mix powdered sugar, cream cheese and Cool Whip; spread on cooled crust. Mix pudding according to directions on box and spread on cream cheese. Top with remaining Cool Whip and you can grate Hershey's Chocolate Bar on top. Refrigerate before serving.

Banana Cream Pie
Selected

3/4 c. sugar	2 Tbs. margarine
1/3 c. all purpose flour	1 tsp. vanilla extract
1/4 tsp. salt	1 baked pie shell (9 inch)
2 c. milk	3 medium firm bananas
3 egg yolks, lightly beaten	Whipped cream & sliced bananas

In a saucepan combine sugar, flour and salt; stir in milk and mix well. Cook over medium heat, stirring constantly, until the mixture thickens and comes to a boil. Boil two minutes. Remove from heat. Stir in a small amount into egg yolks. Return all to saucepan. Cook for two minutes, stirring constantly. Remove from heat. Add butter and vanilla; cool slightly. Slice the bananas into pastry shell, pour filling over, and cool. Before serving you may add whipped topping and more sliced bananas.

Banana Pudding
Selected

1 can condensed milk	2 c. whipped cream or 1 large Cool
1 1/2 c. cold water	Whip
1 small pkg. instant vanilla	3 bananas
pudding mix	Vanilla wafers (approximately 35)

In large bowl, combine condensed milk and water; add pudding mix and beat well. Chill about five minutes; fold in whipped cream. Spoon 1 c. pudding mixture into a 2 1/2 quart glass bowl and top with 1/3 wafers, 1/3 bananas and pudding. Repeat layers. Chill.

Old Fashioned Banana Pudding
Madeline Darnell, Sulphur, LA

1 c. sugar
6 heaping Tbs. (self-rising) flour
2 eggs
3 1/2 c. skim or regular milk

2 very ripe bananas
1 tsp. vanilla
4 ripe bananas
1 pkg. vanilla wafers

In a saucepan, mix sugar and flour. Add eggs and slowly mix in 1/2 c. milk until mixed well. Slowly add rest of milk. Cook over low heat until mixture thickens, stirring constantly. Add two very ripe mashed bananas and vanilla. Mix well. Add the rest of bananas that have been sliced. Line large bowl with wafers; add layer of pudding, more wafers, then mixture, etc., until pudding is used up.

Eclair Dessert
Selected

2 (3 3/4 oz.) French vanilla
instant pudding
1 (16 oz.) box graham crackers

3 c. cold milk
1 (12 oz.) whipped topping
1 can chocolate icing

Layer whole crackers in bottom of 9 x 12 inch pan. Mix pudding and milk. Fold in whipped topping. Put half of pudding mixture on crackers. Add another layer of crackers and cover with rest of pudding. Top with layer of crackers and cover with chocolate icing. Chill and keep refrigerated.

Tapioca Pudding
Selected

4 pkg. (3 oz.) tapioca pudding
4 c. milk
16 oz. frozen whipped topping, thawed
2 cans (22 oz.) lemon pie filling

1 pkg. (10 1/2 oz.) miniature marshmallows
4 cans (15 oz.) mandarin oranges, drained
20 oz.can crushed pineapple, drained
4 cans (17 oz.) fruit cocktail, drained

In a large saucepan, cook pudding and milk according to package directions. Cool. In a large bowl, fold whipped topping into pie fillings. Add the remaining ingredients; stir gently. Fold in pudding. Refrigerate overnight.

Rice Pudding
Norma Moore, Tyro, NC

3 c. long grained rice, cooked
3/4 c. raisins
2 1/2 c. milk
1 c. sugar

2 tsp. vanilla
1/4 tsp. salt
6 eggs
1/4 tsp. cinnamon

In large bowl, combine rice, raisins, 1 1/2 c. milk, sugar, vanilla and salt. Set this aside. In a small bowl beat remaining cup of milk and eggs until thoroughly blended. Stir into rice mixture. Pour into 2 or 3 quart casserole dish. Bake at 350° for 30 minutes. Stir gently and dust with cinnamon. Continue to bake 30 to 40 more minutes more until lightly browned and set.

Pumpkin Whip
Selected

1 pkg. instant butterscotch
  pudding (3.4 oz.)
1 1/2 c. cold milk

1 c. canned pumpkin
1 tsp. pumpkin pie spice
1 1/2 c. whipped topping

In a mixing bowl, beat pudding and milk until well blended. Blend in pumpkin and pie spice. Fold in whipped topping. Spoon into dessert dishes and chill. Yields 6 servings.

Squash Pie
Rosella Rowe, Lexington, NC

1 c. brown sugar
2 c. milk
1 c. white sugar
4 eggs, beaten
2 c. cooked squash

2 Tbs. flour
1 tsp. nutmeg
1 tsp. cinnamon
1 tsp. salt
2 pie shells

Combine sugars and milk first; then add all other ingredients. Pour into unbaked pie shell and bake at 425° for 10 minutes; then reduce heat to 350° and continue to bake until done.

Cow Pies
Selected

12 oz. milk chocolate chips	1/2 c. raisins
1 Tbs. shortening	1/2 c. chopped slivered almonds

In a double boiler over simmering water, melt the chocolate chips and shortening, stirring until smooth. Remove from heat and stir in raisins and almonds. Drop by tablespoonfuls onto waxed paper. Chill. Yields 2 dozen.

Strawberry Pie
Selected

3 quarts fresh strawberries, divided	1 c. heavy cream
	1/2 Tbs. instant vanilla pudding mix
1/2 c. sugar	Deep dish pastry shell
6 Tbs. cornstarch	Red food coloring (optional)
2/3 c. water	

In a large bowl, mash enough berries to equal 3 cups. In a saucepan, combine the sugar and cornstarch. Stir in mashed berries and water; mix well. Bring to a boil over medium heat, stirring constantly. Cook and stir for 2 minutes. Remove from heat and add food coloring if desired. Pour into large bowl. Chill for 20 minutes, stirring occasionally until mixture is just slightly warm. Fold in the remaining berries. Pile into pie shell. Chill for 1 -3 hours. In a small mixing bowl whip cream until soft peaks form. Sprinkle pudding mix over cream and whip until stiff. This makes wonderful topping.

Fresh Strawberry Pie
Norma Moore, Tyro, NC

Mix together:

3 Tbs. dry wild strawberry Jell-O	3 Tbs. cornstarch
	1 c. water
1 c. sugar	2 or 3 drops of food coloring

Cook all the above until clear and thick. Cool. Pour into a baked 9 in. cooled pie shell, piled with strawberries.

133

Fruit & Nut Cherry Pie

Selected

1 can (21 oz.) cherry pie filling
1 can (20 oz) crushed pineapple, undrained
3/4 c. sugar
1 Tbs. cornstarch

1 tsp. red food coloring, opt.
4 medium firm bananas, sliced
1/2 c. chopped pecans
2 pastry shells (9 inch) baked
Whipped cream

In a saucepan, combine pie filling, pineapple, sugar, cornstarch and food coloring and mix well. Bring to a boil over medium heat, stirring constantly. Cook and stir for two minutes. Cool. Fold in bananas and nuts. Pour into pie shells. Chill. Garnish with whipped cream. Must be refrigerated.

Butterscotch Pie

Ruby Pickens, Canton, NC

1 1/2 c. brown sugar
4 1/2 Tbs. butter
6 Tbs. cream
Pinch of salt

1 1/2 c. milk
9 Tbs. flour
2 egg yolks

Cook sugar, butter and cream until thick and brown. The browner it is cooked the more butterscotch taste it has. Mix the milk, flour, egg yolks and salt. Stir into the first mixture, stirring constantly. Cook until thick and pour into baked pie crust.

Lemon Chess Pie

Norma Moore, Tyro, NC

1 1/4 c. sugar
3 lg. eggs
1 stick butter, softened

1 Tbs. vinegar
1 tsp. lemon extract

Mix ingredients and beat thoroughly until fluffy (use spoon). Do not use mixer. Bake in uncooked pie shell for 30 to 35 minutes at 325^0. Makes one pie.

Angel Food Pie

Ruby Pickens, Canton, NC

1 1/2 c. sugar
9 Tbs. cornstarch
3 c. boiling water
3 beaten egg whites
Pinch of salt

1 c. crushed pineapple
1 tsp. vanilla
1 tsp. lemon
Baked pie crust

Cook sugar, cornstarch and boiling water until thick and clear. Beat egg whites and add to liquid, adding salt, pineapple, vanilla and lemon flavorings. Pour in baked crust and let set until cool.
Note: You may add whipped cream to top.

CANDY
Cinnamon Candy Popcorn

Kim Patterson, Emporia, VA

8 qts. plain popped popcorn
1 c. butter

1/2 c. light corn syrup
1 pkg. (9 oz.) red-hot candies

Place popcorn in a large bowl and set aside. In a saucepan, combine butter, corn syrup and candies. Bring to a boil over medium heat, stirring constantly. Boil for 5 minutes, stirring occasionally. Pour over popcorn and mix thoroughly. Turn into 2 greased 15 x 10 baking pans. Bake at 250^0 for 1 hour, stirring every 15 minutes. Remove from pans and place on waxed paper to cool. Break apart; store in air tight container or plastic bags.

Fudge

Betty Thomas, Greenville, NC

10 Tbs. hot water
8 Tbs. cocoa
1 Tbs. vanilla
1 stick margarine

1 1/2 box powdered sugar,
    (more if needed)
Nuts

Boil water, mix with cocoa, vanilla, and margarine until dissolved. Add powdered sugar and nuts. Put in buttered platter; let stand in refrigerator, if desired.

Velveeta Cheese Fudge
Kathy De Foor, Godley, TX

1 lb. Velveeta cheese	4 lb. confectioners sugar
1 lb. margarine	1 c. cocoa
1 Tbs. vanilla	6 c. pecans

Heat until melted: cheese, margarine and vanilla. Meanwhile, combine confectioners sugar, cocoa and pecans. Combine the two mixtures, using hands. When completely mixed, spread into two 13 x 9 buttered pans. Chill for one hour and slice. Freeze well. Note: You can melt the cheese, butter and vanilla in the microwave or a double boiler.

Buttermilk Fudge
Donna Lisenbee, Boaz, AL

1 c. buttermilk	3 Tbs. light Karo syrup
1 tsp. soda	1 tsp. vanilla
2 c. sugar	1 c. nuts

Add soda to buttermilk and let stand for at least 5 minutes. Add sugar & syrup and cook until it reaches the soft ball stage of 238^0. Remove from heat and cool until lukewarm. Add vanilla and nuts; beat until it begins to thickens and loses its glossy color.

White Fudge
Selected

1 c. margarine	1 (7 oz.) marshmallow cream
1 can evaporated milk	1 c. chopped walnuts
4 c. sugar	1 tsp. vanilla
1 (12 oz.) pkg. white candy wafers	

Let margarine begin to melt in heavy saucepan. Brush sides of pan with melted margarine. Add sugar and milk. Mix and cook over medium heat to boiling, stirring continuously to dissolve sugar. Cook to soft ball stage, about 12 to 15 minutes. Remove from heat and add candy wafers and marshmallow cream. Stir until blended. Add walnuts and vanilla. Pour into buttered dish.

Microwave Fudge

Kate Cravatt, Brewton, AL

1/4 c. cocoa	2 c. sugar
1 can Carnation milk	18 oz. marshmallow cream
2 c. brown sugar	1 stick margarine
18 oz. peanut butter	

Cook on high in microwave for 16 - 20 minutes, turning 1/4 turn every 4 minutes.

Hard Candy

Maddy Ray, Tempe, AZ

2 c. sugar	1 c. water
3/4 c. white corn syrup	

Boil until 300^0 degrees (hard crack). Remove and add flavor of your choice. Color with food coloring. Pour in well buttered pan and cut with scissors. Note: You have to work fast.

Quick Caramels

Betty Midkiff, Salt Rock, WV

1 c. butter	1 c. light corn syrup
1 lb. pkg. brown sugar	1 14 oz. can sweetened condensed milk
Dash of salt	1 tsp. vanilla

Butter 9 x 9 x 2 pan. Melt butter in heavy saucepan; add sugar and salt. Stir thoroughly. Stir in corn syrup. Gradually add sweetened condensed milk stirring constantly. Clip candy thermometer in pan. Bring to 245^0. Remove from heat. Stir in vanilla. Pour into buttered pan. Cool, cut and wrap in wax paper. Makes 2 1/2 Pounds.

Old-Fashioned Peanut Brittle

Elsie Gilkerson, Milton, FL

1 c. peanuts	1/2 tsp. cream of tartar
1/2 c. water	1 Tbs. vinegar
1 c. light brown sugar	2 Tbs. butter

Grease a cookie sheet with butter. Spread peanuts and set aside. Mix together water, brown sugar, cream of tartar and vinegar. Boil for 10 minutes; then add butter and continue boiling until mixture dropped in cold water hardens like glass. Take from heat and pour over peanuts. When cool, break into pieces.

Seafoam Candy

Selected

1 box brown sugar	2 lg. egg whites
1/2 c. water	1 tsp. vanilla

Boil sugar and water on medium until it spins a thread 4 inches long. While this is cooking, beat egg whites until very stiff. Add cooked syrup very slowly, continuing beating at all times. Beat until the mixture becomes dull; add vanilla. Spoon onto wax paper.

Divinity

Selected

2 c. sugar	2 egg whites
1/2 c. white Karo syrup	1 tsp. vanilla
1/2 c. water	1 c. chopped pecans

Combine Karo, water and sugar in a saucepan. Boil at 265^0. Beat egg whites stiff in a mixing bowl and gradually beat in the boiling syrup. Beat until it begins to be stiff. Add vanilla and nuts. Beat again and pour into a buttered dish. Cut as you desire.

Pecan Pralines
Selected

1 c. sugar	1 c. pecans, chopped
1/2 c. evaporated milk	1 c. brown sugar
2 Tbs. margarine	1 tsp. vanilla

Mix ingredients in a saucepan. Let boil until it forms a soft ball in cold water, approximately five minutes. Drop by spoonfuls on waxed paper.

Peanut Butter Marshmallow Fudge
Selected

2 c. sugar	1 c. peanut butter
1/2 c. milk	1 c. marshmallow cream

Combine sugar and milk. Boil until it forms a soft ball in cold water. Remove from heat. Add peanut butter and marshmallow cream. Beat until smooth. Pour onto greased plate. Cut when cooled.

Turtles
Selected

60 Kraft caramels	12 oz. bag of chocolate chips
1/2 c. whipping cream	1 block paraffin
4 c. pecans (finely chopped)	

Melt caramels and whipping cream. Add pecans. Drop by spoonfuls onto greased cookie sheet. Freeze until hard. Melt chocolate chips and paraffin in a double boiler. Dip turtles in by toothpicks and place on wax paper. Keep refrigerated.

Potato Candy

Selected

1 medium potato (peeled and cut-up)
1/8 tsp. vanilla
2 lg. bags powdered sugar
Peanut butter

Boil potato, drain. Let cool and mash. Add powdered sugar till it thickens enough to roll out as a dough. Spread a piece of wax paper; sprinkle with powdered sugar and roll potato dough out on paper with a roller. Shape into a large triangle (not too thin). Spread a layer of peanut butter all over the dough. Begin rolling from point of triangle upward. Wrap wax paper with sugar around roll; then with foil. Chill overnight. Cut into 1/4 inch slices.

Potato Candy

Donna Lisenbee, Boaz, AL

1 medium potato peeled & boiled   1 tsp. peppermint flavoring
2 1/2 - 3 1/2 c. powdered sugar

Mash hot potatoes thoroughly. Add sugar slowly until a rolled dough stage. Add flavoring. (Taste to see if you need to add more sugar or flavoring.) Roll in wax paper, after spreading on wax paper, until 1/4 inch, then refrigerate. Slice into pieces of candy.

Coconut Balls

Selected

2 boxes powdered sugar
1 stick margarine, softened
1 can Eagle Brand milk
1 c. chopped pecans

1 can coconut
12 oz. chocolate chips
1/2 cake paraffin wax

Mix sugar, milk and butter. Add coconut and pecans. Roll into small balls. Place in freezer. Melt chocolate chips and wax in double boiler. Dip balls and place on wax paper until dry.

Millionaire Candy
Dorothy Grady, Mt.Olive, NC

16 oz. Kraft caramels
1 can Eagle Brand milk

3 c. chopped pecans
12 oz. block style chocolate

Melt caramels until smooth in microwave; add milk and pecans. Drop onto greased cookie sheet and put in freezer for about 1 hour. Melt chocolate in microwave and dip candy in chocolate with tongs; drop onto wax paper.

Peppermint Patties
Kim Patterson, Emporia, VA

1 box confectioners sugar
3 Tbs. butter, softened
2 to 3 tsp. peppermint extract
1/2 tsp. vanilla extract

1/4 c. evaporated milk
2 c. semi-sweet chocolate chips
2 Tbs. shortening

In a bowl, combine first four ingredients. Add milk and mix well. Roll into 1 in. balls & place on a waxed paper lined cookie sheet. Chill for 20 minutes. Flatten with a glass to 1/4 in. and chill for 30 minutes. In a double boiler or microwave, melt chocolate chips and shortening. Dip patties and place on waxed paper to harden. Yields 5 dozen.

FROSTINGS
Vanilla Frosting
Mary Fellure, Milton, FL

1 lb. confectioners sugar
1 c. Crisco
1/4 c. milk

1 tsp. colorless vanilla
2 tsp. butter flavoring

Mix all ingredients well and spread on favorite cake.

Cream Cheese Frosting

Chris Perrine, Milton, FL

8 oz. cream cheese, softened
1 tsp. vanilla

1/2 stick margarine, softened
1 lb. confectioners sugar

Cream margarine and cheese. Add sugar and vanilla and beat well.

Cream Cheese Frosting

Madeline Darnell, Sulphur, LA

8 oz. cream cheese, softened
1 stick margarine, softened
1 box confectioners sugar

1 tsp. vanilla
1 c. chopped nuts
1 c. coconut

Mix first four ingredients, then add nuts and coconut. Spread.

Decorator Icing

Sandy Skipper, North, SC

3 lbs. powdered sugar, sifted
1/4 to 1/3 can Crisco
1/2 c. tap water

1 Tbs. clear vanilla
1 Tbs. almonds
1 Tbs. orange*

*Or strawberry, lemon. coconut, butter, or chocolate flavoring
Mix well using a small hand mixer. Icing has better consistency if mixed up
24 hours before and allowing to sit (air bubbles escape). Restir with a spoon
before use. Note: Cover bowl with wet towel after mixing.

Decorator Icing

Selected

1 1/2 c. Crisco
2 tsp. white Karo syrup
1 tsp. butter
1 tsp. vanilla

1 tsp. almond
1 tsp. butter extract
1/2 c. water
1 lb. confectioners sugar

Mix all ingredients at medium speed, except water and sugar. Blend until
well creamed. Add water and sugar and mix well.

Seven-Minute Frosting
Mary Fellure, Milton, FL

2 egg whites
1 1/2 c. sugar
5 Tbs. cold water

1 1/2 tsp. light corn syrup
1 tsp. vanilla

Put unbeaten egg whites, sugar, water, and corn syrup in upper part of a double boiler. Place over rapidly boiling water. Beat constantly with rotary beater for 7 to 10 minutes. Remove from heat; add vanilla. Beat until thick enough to spread. Makes enough to fill and frost a 2 layer cake.

Italian Cream Cheese Frosting
Selected

8 oz. cream cheese, softened
1 stick butter, softened
1 lb. confectioners sugar
1 tsp. vanilla extract

1/2 c. crushed pineapple
1/2 c. pecans, chopped
1/2 c. coconut

Cream butter and cream cheese. Add remaining ingredients.

Mocha Frosting
Letha Ray, Salt Rock, WV

1/3 c. butter or margarine
3 c. confectioners sugar
1/4 c. strong, cold coffee

2 squares unsweetened chocolate, melted

Cream butter or margarine to consistency of mayonnaise. Add half the sugar gradually while continuing to cream. Add chocolate and mix well. Add remaining sugar. Add coffee, 1 Tbs. at a time until frosting is fluffy and easy to spread. Makes enough to fill and frost a 2 layer cake.

Peanut Butter Frosting
Selected

1/2 c. butter, softened
3 c. powdered sugar
1/2 c. peanut butter

3 Tbs. milk
1 tsp. vanilla

Combine butter, sugar and peanut butter until smooth. Add vanilla and milk. Add more milk if needed for smooth consistency.

Walnut Frosting
Selected

2 Tbs. margarine
1 c. lt. brown sugar
2 Tbs. plain flour

1 tsp. cinnamon
1/2 c. walnuts, chopped

With wooden spoon or hands, mix all ingredients. This mixture is crumbly so spread evenly over cake. Brown in oven for 8 to 10 minutes.

Pecan Coconut Frosting
Letha Ray, Salt Rock, WV

1 c. evaporated milk
1 c. sugar
3 egg yolks
1/2 c. margarine

1 tsp. vanilla
1 1/3 c. coconut
1 c. pecans, chopped

Cook and stir all ingredients, except coconut and nuts, over medium heat about 12 minutes. Add coconut and nuts. Beat until thick enough to spread.

Pretzel Candy
Selected

1 lb. white chocolate
2 c. skinny pretzels

1 can salted peanuts

Melt chocolate over medium heat. Stir in pretzels and peanuts. Let stand a little while. Drop by teaspoon onto wax paper.

Fluffy Cocoa Frosting
Selected

3/4 c. Hershey's Cocoa
4 c. confectioners sugar
1/2 c. margarine, softened

1/2 c. evaporated milk
1 tsp. vanilla

Mix cocoa and sugar. Cream part of the cocoa-sugar mixture with the margarine. Blend in vanilla and half of the milk. Add remaining cocoa to the sugar mixture and blend well. Add remaining milk and beat to a spreading consistency.

Orange Coconut Frosting
Selected

1 c. sugar
4 Tbs. cornstarch
1/4 tsp. salt
2 Tbs. orange rind
Coconut to cover cake

1 c. water
1 Tbs. lemon juice
2 eggs, beaten
2 Tbs. butter

Mix sugar, cornstarch and salt. Add remaining ingredients and cook until thick. Cover with coconut.

Chocolate Frosting
Selected

3 oz. unsweetened chocolate
2 c. sugar
1/2 c. Crisco

2/3 c. milk
1/2 tsp. salt
1 tsp. vanilla

Mix all ingredients except vanilla. In saucepan heat to boiling, stirring occasionally. Boil for 1 minute without stirring. Place pan in bowl of ice water. Beat until smooth. Stir in vanilla.

Buttermilk Icing
Selected

1 c. sugar
1/2 c. buttermilk
1/2 tsp. baking soda

1/2 stick margarine
1 tsp. vanilla

Mix well and bring to a boil over low heat, stirring constantly. Add vanilla.

Pistachio Frosting
Selected

1 envelope Dream Whip
1 pkg. pistachio pudding
1/2 tsp. almond extract

1 c. cold milk
1 small container of Cool Whip

Beat all ingredients, except Cool Whip until stiff. Fold in Cool Whip. You may use extra green food coloring if desired.

Never Fail Meringue
Selected

1 Tbs. cornstarch
2 Tbs. cold water
1/2 c. boiling water
3 egg whites

6 Tbs. sugar
Dash of salt
1/2 tsp. vanilla

Blend cornstarch and cold water in saucepan. Add boiling water and cook until clear and thick. Let cool. Beat egg whites until foamy. Gradually add sugar and beat until stiff. Add salt and vanilla and cool mixture. Beat well. Bake at 350^0 for 10 minutes. Make sure your pie is completely cool before spreading on the meringue.

146

German Sweet Chocolate Frosting

Selected

1 c. sugar
1 c. evaporated milk
1 c. coconut
1 c. chopped pecans

3 egg yolks
1 stick margarine
1 tsp. vanilla

Cook all ingredients until thick. Spread on hot cake.

The most expensive vehicle to operate, per mile, is the shopping cart.

Miscellaneous

Sugar-Free Strawberry Jam
Selected

3/4 c. diet lemon-lime soda   1 1/2 tsp. lemon juice
1 pkg. (3 oz) sugar-free strawberry gelatin
1 c. mashed fresh or frozen strawberries.

In a saucepan, bring soda to a boil. Remove from the heat and stir in gelatin until dissolved. Stir in strawberries and lemon juice. Pour into jars; cover and refrigerate up to 3 weeks. Do not freeze.

Fruit Juice Jelly
Selected

4 c. unsweetened grape juice   1 (1 3/4 oz.) pkg. powdered fruit pectin
1/4 c. lemon juice   4 1/2 c. sugar

Pour grape juice and lemon juice into a kettle. Sprinkle with pectin. Let stand 1 to 2 hours; stir to dissolve. Bring to a full rolling boil over medium-high heat, stirring frequently. Stir in sugar. Return to full rolling boil; stir often. Boil hard 1 minute, stirring constantly. Remove from heat and quickly skim off foam with a metal spoon. Ladle into hot sterilized jars, leaving 1/4 inch headspace. Adjust lids.

Oven Baked Apple Butter
Selected

5 qt. applesauce, unsweetened   3 tsp. cinnamon
4 c. sugar   1/2 tsp. nutmeg
4 c. brown sugar   1 tsp. cloves
1 c. cider or vinegar   1/4 tsp. allspice

Core, cut and cook 7 pounds of apples until soft and press through food mill to make applesauce. Combine applesauce and next three ingredients and cook in 350° oven for about four hours or until thick, stirring occasionally. After 3 1/2 hours, add spices. Pour into sterilized jars and seal.

Heavenly Jam
Selected

5 c. rhubarb, diced
5 c. sugar

1 (20 oz.) can crushed pineapple
1 lg. box strawberry Jell-O

Combine, rhubarb, sugar and crushed pineapple. Stir to blend. Boil hard for 20 minutes. Remove from stove. Add Jell-O and stir well to dissolve. As soon as Jell-O melts, put into sterilized jars and seal.

Fried Apples
Selected

6 medium apples, peeled and sliced
1/4 c. butter
1/2 c. sugar

Heat butter in a heavy skillet. Just before butter starts to brown add apples and sugar. Fry until golden brown.

Fried Apple Pies
Marie St. John, Burlington, NC

1 lb. dried apples
Sweeten to taste

Nutmeg & cinnamon to taste
10 count can of biscuits

Soak and wash apples and cook until tender. Add sugar and spices. Roll out each biscuit. Put apples in middle and pinch the edges so as not to leak out. Cook in hot shortening until brown. Drain.

Glazed Apples
Selected

4 large apples
1/2 c. sugar

1/2 tsp. cinnamon
1 c. water

Core whole, unpaired apples; slit peel around middle of each apple. Mix sugar and cinnamon together; fill centers of apples. Put apples in saucepan; add water and cover. Cook for 25 minutes until tender, spooning liquid over them occasionally. Remove cover during last minute of cooking.

Sweetened Condensed Milk
Selected

1 c. instant dry milk
2/3 c. sugar

1/3 c. boiling water
3 Tbs. butter

Combine all ingredients in container in electric blender; process until smooth. Store in refrigerator. Yields about 1 1/4 c.

Egg Beaters
Selected

4 unbeaten egg whites
1 Tbs. oil

1 Tbs. dry milk
3 drops yellow food coloring

Combine all ingredients and mix well.

Chocolate Covered Pecans
Betty Thomas, Greenville, NC

4 c. pecans
12 oz. semisweet chocolate chips

Melt enough margarine to rub into pecans. Toast them in oven at 325^0, stirring 2 or 3 times just until crispy. Remove from oven. Melt chocolate chips over double boiler and put pecans into the hot chocolate. Mix, turning them over and over until it gets cool and stiff. Spread pecans on wax paper. Will cool quickly.

Knox Blox
Selected

4 envelopes Knox
4 c. boiling water

3 pkgs. (3 oz.) Jell-O

In a bowl combine Knox and Jell-O. Add boiling water and stir. Pour into pan and chill.

Vegetable Relish

Lillian Miller, Murfreesboro, TN

2 cans English peas (drained)
2 cans Mexi-corn
2 jars pimentoes

2 lg. onions (chopped)
2 c. chopped celery

Mix, cover and refrigerate.

Dressing
2 c. sugar
2 c. vinegar

Mix well and pour over vegetables. Refrigerate. Keeps well.

Ranch Dressing

Betty Midkiff, Salt Rock, WV

1 c. mayonnaise
1 c. buttermilk
1 tsp. garlic salt
1 tsp. parsley flakes

1 Tbs. minced dry onion
1/4 tsp. Accent
1/8 tsp. pepper

Mix all ingredients and let set a few hours before serving.
Note: You can use sweet milk.

Italian Dressing

Letha Ray, Salt Rock, WV

1 c. Crisco oil
1/3 c. vinegar
2 Tbs. lemon juice
1 tsp. garlic salt

1 tsp. sugar
1/2 tsp. dry mustard
1/2 tsp. oregano
Black pepper

Combine in shaker jar and chill.

Pickled Squash
Mary Fellure, Milton, FL

Slice thin:
8 c. yellow squash   1 c. onions
1 bell pepper

Place in pan, sprinkle with handful of salt; let stand one hour. Drain on paper towel and blot excess moisture.

Bring to boil:
2 c. vinegar   2 tsp. mustard seed
3 c. sugar   2 tsp. celery seed

When vinegar mixture reaches a hard boil add squash, onion and pepper mixture and bring to a boil again. Place in hot sterile jars and seal. Note: Tastes like cucumber pickles.

Microwave Caramel Corn
Maddy Ray, Tempe, AZ

1/2 c. brown sugar   1/2 tsp. baking soda
1/2 c. margarine   3 c. popped popcorn
1/2 c. Karo syrup

Put the first three ingredients in microwave dish and cook on high 2 minutes (or until margarine is melted). Stir and return to microwave 2 more minutes. Add soda and then stir. Put popcorn in a large brown bag and pour caramel mixture on top. Mix with spoon to coat popcorn. Fold top down, shake, then microwave another 1 1/2 minutes. Shake bag, and microwave another 1 1/2 minutes. Shake and microwave another 45 seconds.

Sweet & Sour Salad Dressing
Faye Chapman, Milton, WV

1/3 c. lime or lemon juice   1 1/2 tsp. brown sugar
1/3 c. water

Mix ingredients together in small bowl.

153

Dijon Salad Dressing
Iva Gilkerson, Huntington, WV

1/4 c. Dijon mustard
1/2 c. water

1 tsp. basil
1 tsp. oregano

Mix ingredients together in small bowl.

Tartar Sauce
Selected

1 pt. mayonnaise
1/2 c. sweet relish

1/2 c. chopped onions
1 oz. sweet pickle juice

Stir mayonnaise until there are no lumps. Mix all ingredients well in mayonnaise

Beignets
Anne Fuller, Grovetown, GA

1 c. flour
1/2 tsp. salt
1 well beaten egg

2 tsp. baking powder
1/2 c. milk

Mix egg and milk; gradually add flour mixture and mix well. Drop by tsp. in hot oil. Cook until lightly browned, about two minutes. Drain on paper towel and roll in cinnamon/sugar or powered sugar.

Sweet Pickles
Dorothy Grady, Mt. Olive, NC

1 qt. cucumbers
1 tsp. salt
1 tsp. alum

1/4 tsp. turmeric
1 tsp. whole pickling spice
Cold vinegar

Slice one quart of cucumbers and pack in jar. Add salt, alum, turmeric and whole pickling spice. Fill jar with cold vinegar and cover. Let stand for 60 days or indefinitely. Three or more days before you want to eat them, pour off vinegar and add 2 cups sugar. Put spices in bag.

Freezer Cucumber Pickles
Selected

4 lbs. cucumbers, sliced
8 c. thinly sliced onions
1/4 c. salt

3/4 c. water
4 c. sugar
2 c. cider vinegar

Combine cucumbers, onions, salt and water in two large bowls. Let stand at room temperature for two hours. Add sugar and vinegar, stir until sugar dissolves. Pack into 1 pint freezer containers, leaving 1 inch headspace. Cover and freeze up to 6 weeks. Thaw at room temperature before serving. Yields 10 pints.

Faye's Pickles
Faye Chapman, Milton, WV

7 c. sliced cucumbers
2 bell peppers (sliced)
2 onions (sliced)
1 Tbs. salt

1 tsp. celery seed
2 c. sugar
1 c. vinegar

Mix all ingredients and cover overnight. Keep refrigerated.

Play Doh
Selected

3 Tbs. oil
2 c. boiling water
Food coloring

3 1/2 c. flour
1/2 c. salt
1 Tbs. alum

Combine oil, boiling water, and food coloring. Add dry ingredients. Knead until thoroughly mixed.

Scrambled Eggs

Elsie Gilkerson, Milton, FL

4 eggs
1/4 c. milk
1/2 tsp. salt

1/2 tsp. pepper
1 Tbs. butter

Mix eggs, milk, salt and pepper with fork. Heat butter in skillet and stir in egg mixture. Reduce heat enough to cook egg mixture quickly, lifting from bottom and sides as mixture thickens. Cook until eggs are thickened, but moist.

Cheese Grits

Selected

6 c. water
1 1/2 c. grits
1 lb. sharp cheddar cheese, grated
3 eggs, beaten
1 1/2 sticks margarine

1 Tbs. seasoned salt
1 tsp. Tabasco sauce
1 tsp. paprika
1 1/2 tsp. salt

Boil water; add grits slowly stirring constantly so they don't lump. Cook at lower temperature for 5 minutes. Add remaining ingredients and bake in buttered casserole dish for 1 hour at 350⁰.

Breakfast Sausage and Egg Casserole

Vicki Richburg, Six Mile, SC

1 pkg. sausage
6 eggs
2 c. milk
1 tsp. salt

1 tsp. dry mustard
2 slices day old bread, crumbled
1 c. cheddar cheese, grated
2 Tbs. onion, chopped

Brown sausage. Drain. Mix all ingredients together and pour into a casserole dish. Bake at 350⁰ for 45 minutes. Serves 6 - 8.

Strawberry Pizza
Faye Chapman, Milton, WV

1 roll of sugar cookie dough	2 c. confectioners sugar
8 oz. Cool Whip	1 package strawberry glaze
8 oz. pkg. of cream cheese	Strawberry slices for top.

Bake sugar cookie dough in pizza pan. Cool. Mix together Cool Whip, cream cheese and confectioners sugar. Spread on dough; then add glaze and strawberry slices.

Cake Crumb Coating
Sandy Skipper, North, SC

1/4 c. water	1 1/2 c. decorator icing

Spread thinly over cake. Allow to dry at least one hour before applying the final coat of icing. Note: Used to "glue" the crumbs to the cake so they will not be caught up in final icing.

Cracker Jacks
Lisa Bailes, Summersville, WV

2 c. brown sugar	1/2 c. Karo syrup
2 sticks margarine	

Boil 1 minute. Pour over 2 gallons of popped popcorn. Stir, then bake 1 hour at 250^0 stirring every 15 minutes.

Freezer Ice Cream
Selected

1 c. evaporated milk	3 or 4 eggs
2 c. sugar	1 tsp. vanilla

Mix eggs and sugar; cream evaporated milk and vanilla together. Put in freezer and freeze according to freezer directions.

Hot Apple Cider
Selected

2/3 c. brown sugar
1 tsp. whole cloves
1 tsp. allspice

3 cinnamon sticks, broken
1 gallon apple cider

Fill the filter-lined basket of a large automatic percolator with brown sugar, cloves, allspice and cinnamon sticks. Prepare as you would coffee, but substitute apple cider instead of water. Note: Do not use drip style coffeemaker.

Egg Nog
Selected

1 dozen eggs
1 1/2 c. white sugar
2 qt. milk

1/2 gal. vanilla ice cream
12 oz. Cool Whip
Nutmeg

Separate egg yolks from whites. Beat egg yolks until fluffy. Add 1 c. sugar; beat until sugar is dissolved. While still beating, add milk. To this mixture beat in ice cream. Fold in Cool Whip. Set aside in a separate bowl. Beat egg whites until stiff. Add 1/2 c. sugar to egg whites and beat until smooth. Top liquid mixture with egg white mixture and sprinkle with nutmeg.

Breakfast Casserole
Marie St. John, Burlington, NC

1 box Pepperidge Farm
  seasoned croutons
1 lb. browned sausage, drained

1 lb. grated cheddar cheese
8 eggs
1 pt. half & half

Beat eggs and half & half. Line croutons, sausage and cheese, in that order. Then add egg-milk mixture. Cover and refrigerate overnight. Next morning, bake at 350⁰ for 30 minutes.

Breakfast Sausage Scramble

Marie St. John, Burlington, NC

1 lb. sausage	1/2 c. chopped onion
3 Tbs. butter	2 c. boiled potatoes, diced
2 Tbs. all-purpose flour	

Brown sausage in heavy skillet. Drain. Blend butter and flour; add onions and potatoes. Cook slowly for 10 minutes. Add milk; cook 5 minutes or until mixture thickens, stirring constantly.

Waffles

Selected

2 1/4 c. sifted all-purpose flour	2 eggs, beaten
4 tsp. baking powder	2 1/4 c. milk
3/4 tsp. salt	1/2 c. vegetable oil
1 1/2 tsp. sugar	

Mix dry ingredients together. Add liquid ingredients all at once, beating only until moistened. Bake in preheated waffle iron. Makes 12.

Deviled Eggs

Mary Fellure, Milton, Fl.

6 eggs, boiled	Salt & pepper to taste
1 Tbs. mayonnaise	2 Tbs. relish, more if desired
1 tsp. mustard	

Boil eggs for ten minutes. Let cool; peel and cut in halves. Scoop out egg yolks into a bowl. Add mayonnaise, mustard, relish, salt & pepper. Mix well. Fill each egg half with mixture. Sprinkle top with paprika.

Homemade Frozen Custard
Selected

4 c. milk
4 eggs
1 1/4 c. sugar
1/3 c. cornstarch

1/8 tsp. salt
1 c. sweetened condensed milk
2 Tbs. vanilla

In heavy saucepan, bring milk to a boil. In the meantime, beat eggs and add sugar, cornstarch and salt. Mix very well. Gradually add hot milk and return to the stove. Cook and stir constantly for 6 to 8 minutes or until mixture thickens. Gradually stir in condensed milk and vanilla. Chill for 3 to 4 hours. Pour into ice cream freezer and make as you would normally.

Unleavened Bread
Selected

1/2 c. plain flour
1/2 c. lard
1 1/2 tsp. salt

1 Tbs. sugar
4 or 5 Tbs. water

Roll out, pinch with fork. Cut in squares. Bake at 350° for 10 minutes.

Fruit Whip
Selected

2 egg whites
1/2 c. powdered sugar

1 c. fruit pulp

Beat egg whites until stiff. Add sugar gradually while beating. Fold in pulp. Makes four servings.
Note: May use crushed berries, peaches, applesauce, or apricot pulp.

Orange Julius
Selected

6 oz. orange juice concentrate
1/2 c. water
1 c. milk

10 - 12 ice cubes
3 Tbs. sugar
1/2 tsp. vanilla

Add all ingredients to blender and blend until smooth. Serve immediately.
Yields 8 oz.

Protein Drink
Selected

1 raw egg
1 tsp. wheat germ
1 Tbs. honey
8 oz. plain yogurt

1 1/2 Tbs. powdered milk
1 banana
1 lemon

Mix all ingredients in blender and blend on high for several minutes, then
serve.

Strawberry Slush
Selected

6 oz. strawberry banana gelatin
2 c. boiling water
2 c. cold water
12 oz. frozen orange juice
Sugar to taste

36 oz. pineapple juice
16 oz. lemon juice
36 oz. Hawaiian Punch
1 pkg. strawberry Kool-aide
2 - 4 cans ginger ale

Dissolve fruit gelatin in boiling water. Cool and add remaining ingredients,
except ginger ale. Freeze overnight. When serving, break up slush, pour
ginger ale over and serve.

Wassail
Selected

6 c. apple juice
1 stick cinnamon
2 c. pineapple juice

1/4 tsp. nutmeg
3 tsp. lemon juice
1/4 c. honey

Simmer apple juice and cinnamon stick for five minutes. Add remaining ingredients and simmer five more minutes. Serve hot with cinnamon sticks.

Mocha Float
Selected

1 qt. chocolate ice cream
6 c. strong black coffee

1/2 c. whipped cream
Cinnamon to taste

Place a scoop of ice cream in a tall glass. Fill with coffee; top with whipped cream and sprinkle with cinnamon. Serves 6

Watermelon Ice
Selected

2 1/2 c. watermelon chunks,
  seedless
1 c. sugar

1 Tbs. lemon juice
1 pkg. unflavored gelatin
1 c. heavy cream

Puree seeded watermelon chunks. Soften gelatin in 1/4 c. cold watermelon puree. Heat remaining watermelon puree in medium saucepan over low heat until almost boiling. Add softened gelatin-watermelon puree mixture and stir until dissolved. Remove from heat. Add sugar and lemon juice and stir. Chill, stirring occasionally until the mixture drops slowly from spoon. Whip cream and fold in. Turn into custard cups and freeze.

Seek an appetite by hard toil.

-Horace

Whether therefore ye eat or drink, or whatsoever ye do, do
all to the glory of God. I Corinthians 10:31

HINTS FOR LOWERING FATS

- ♥ Include salads with lunch and dinner.

- ♥ Don't put butter or margarine on the table.

- ♥ Use low-fat mayonnaise.

- ♥ Use low-fat creamer for your coffee.

- ♥ Non-stick pans reduce the amount of fat required for cooking.

- ♥ Avoid the following or eat small portions: butter, cooking oil, chicken skin, bacon, sausage, well-marbled meat, hot-dogs, salad dressings, mayonnaise.

- ♥ Measure your servings until you become familiar with the weights.

- ♥ Don't eat eggs more than two times a week, and it is better to poach or boil rather than fry.

- ♥ Use skim milk with cereals.

- ♥ When using margarine on toast, use whipped so it may spread more thinly.

- ♥ Broil, bake, steam or braise meats instead of frying.

- ♥ Try a cup of nonfat yogurt with fruit as a dessert.

- ♥ Add powdered milk to mashed potatoes.

- ♥ Potatoes are not fattening: what you put on them is.

- ♥ Avoid canned or processed tomatoes which are high in sodium.

- ♥ Substitute fresh vegetables and fruits for processed ones.

- ♥ Learn to use spices & herbs for flavoring rather than butter or gravy.

- ♥ Stay away from sugar & coffee & soft drinks containing caffeine.

- ♥ Do not eat within two hours of bedtime.

- ♥ Get into the habit of sipping ice water all day.

INSTANT COOKING REMEDIES

♥ **Lumpy sauce or gravy:**
Pour gravy or sauce through a strainer and mash out lumps with a wooden spoon. Reheat very slowly.

♥ **Stewed fruit is turning sour**:
Add a pinch of baking soda to the fruit and reboil for five minutes.

♥ **Curdled or separated mayonnaise:**
Into warmed bowl, put 1 tsp. mustard, 1 Tbs. curdled mayonnaise. Beat with whisk until creamy.   Add mayonnaise until blended.

♥ **When stewing very sour fruit**:
Add a pinch of salt while stewing to reduce the amount of sugar needed for sweetening.

♥ **Too much fat in gravy**:
Cool the liquid and skim off the fat, or pour through ice cubes into bowl - the fat will solidify and can be removed easily.

♥ **Stored coconut that is dry and hard:**
Put coconut in a strainer over a steaming pot of water for a few minutes.

♥ **A crack in middle of cake**:
The oven was too hot to begin with or temperature was uneven during baking. Disguise crack with icing.

♥ **Hands smell from onion and garlic:**
Rinse hands in cold water, rub with salt or baking powder, rinse again and then wash with soap and water.   .

♥ **Sticky rice**:
Rinse rice thoroughly with warm water to wash out excess starch. Grains will separate.

♥ **Cake has shiny, sticky streak:**
Poor mixing, too slow baking, or irregular heating of pan in oven.

♥ **Shell cracks while egg is boiling:**
Add a few drops of vinegar to the water, use eggs at room temperature.

INSTANT COOKING REMEDIES

♥ **One egg short for recipe**:
Substitute one teaspoon of cornstarch.

♥ **Weak brewed coffee:**
Add a little instant coffee to the pot. It will strengthen it without changing the fresh taste.

♥ **Tough rubbery omelet:**
Add one scant teaspoon of boiling water per egg to mixture to keep omelet from being tough.

♥ **Bitter tasting brewed coffee:**
Put a pinch of salt into the coffee that has brewed too long.

♥ **Weak brewed tea:**
Add a pinch of baking soda to the teapot.

♥ **Slightly stale bread:**
Sprinkle bread with water or milk, wrap in aluminum foil, bake at 350 degrees about 8 minutes. If hard-crusted, open foil for 3-5 minutes more.

♥ **Dry coffeecake:**
Put 2 Tbs. water or milk in large skillet; place uniced cake on trivet. Cover; leave over low heat about 8 minutes. Do not cover iced coffeecake.

♥ **Too much salt:**
Add a little vinegar and sugar, then taste. A raw potato helps absorb salt in soups or stews.

♥ **Fish has strong fishy odor:**
Rub fish with lemon juice and salt to prevent the odor from being absorbed by other food.

♥ **To keep sugar soft and moist:**
Place a slice of bread in the container and cover tightly.

♥ **Dried out leftover cheese:**
Store dried out cheese (unprocessed) in freezer frozen. It crumbles easily; slice it thin without thawing. Use in recipes that call for grated cheese.

♥ **Brown sugar caked and hard:**
Place in 200 degrees oven until the sugar is dry and crumbly. Powder it in an electric blender or use a mortar and pestle.

♥ **Cheese is coated with mold:**
Wipe off mold with paper towel soaked in vinegar. Scrape off heavy mold with knife. Cheese flavor is not affected. Cover lightly with plastic wrap.

♥ **To keep granulated sugar from lumping:**
Place a couple of salt crackers in the container and cover tightly.

♥ **Too much sugar:**
Add a few drops of lemon juice or vinegar.

♥ **Frying fat has strong flavor, odor:**
After frying strong-flavored foods, cool fat. Clarify it by adding a raw potato; reheat slowly, discard potato, strain fat and store.

♥ **Leftover frying fat or oil:**
Cool fat and strain through cheesecloth; store covered in refrigerator.

COOK'S GLOSSARY

♥ **Bake:**
To cook in dry heat.

♥ **Barbecue:**
To roast on a spit or rack over coals.

♥ **Baste:**
To moisten food while cooking by brushing or ladling on melted fat, meat drippings or a sauce.

♥ **Beat:**
To mix vigorously with a rotary beater or electric mixer or with an over and over motion with a spoon.

♥ **Blanch:**
To immerse in boiling water then, in some cases, cold water.

♥ **Blend:**
To mix together 2 or more ingredients so they appear as one unit and will not separate.

♥ **Boil:**
To cook in boiling liquid. Liquid boils when bubbles constantly rise to the surface and break.

♥ **Broil:**
To cook under or over direct heat.

♥ **Brush:**
To cover with melted butter, cream, egg, etc. using a pastry brush, paper or cloth.

♥ **Chop:**
To cut into small pieces with a sharp knife or a chopping bowl and chopper.

♥ **Coat:**
To cover food evenly by rolling in flour, sugar, crumbs, etc. or to dip food in egg or batter.

♥ **Combine:**
To mix all ingredients thoroughly.

COOK'S GLOSSARY

♥ **Cream:**
To beat or stir butter, margarine or shortening and sugar with a spoon or in an electric mixer, until mixture is light and fluffy.

♥ **Cut in shortening:**
To mix shortening and dry ingredients by using 2 knives, scissor-fashion or with a pastry blender until shortening is evenly distributed in small particles.

♥ **Dice:**
To cut into very small cubes.

♥ **Dredge:**
To coat food with flour, sugar, crumbs, etc.

♥ **Flake:**
To break food into small pieces with a fork.

♥ **Fold in:**
To mix, using a gentle down, across, up and over motion usually applied to combining beaten egg whites or whipped cream with another mixture.

♥ **Fry:**
To cook in a little fat, same as sauté or pan fry.

♥ **Glaze:**
To coat with a syrup or jelly mixture.

♥ **Grill:**
Same as broil.

♥ **Marinate**:
To let food, usually meat, stand in a mixture containing acid such as lemon or tomato juice to make meat more tender and to add flavor.

♥ **Mince:**
To cut or chop until very fine.

♥ **Parboil:**
To partly cook food in water preliminary to another method of cooking.

168

COOK'S GLOSSARY

❤ **Pare:**
To cut away outer covering with a knife.

❤ **Peel:**
To pull or slip off outer covering.

❤ **Pit:**
To remove seeds or pits.

❤ **Poach:**
To cook in water kept just below boiling.

❤ **Roast:**
To cook meat or vegetables in oven by dry heat.

❤ **Scald:**
To heat liquid slowly to a temperature just below boiling point until tiny bubbles appear around edge of pan.

❤ **Sear:**
To brown the surface of meat.

❤ **Shred:**
To cut, tear or slice into long thin strips.

❤ **Sift:**
To put dry ingredients through a sieve or flour sifter.

❤ **Simmer:**
To cook in liquid below the boiling point. There should be no bubbling.

❤ **Skewer:**
To hold in place with wooden or metal pins or to thread foods, meat, vegetables and fruits on metal pins.

❤ **Steam:**
To cook surrounded by steam.

❤ **Whip:**
To beat egg whites, creams, etc. with a rotary beater or electric mixer until light and frothy and expanded in volume.

SPICES & HOW TO USE THEM

The term spice as used here includes not only the true spices but also herbs, seeds and blends of spices. Spices provide means of bringing variety to your meals. With the information below, experiment by adding spices to your favorite dishes.

Note: Season with a light hand for subtle flavoring.

♥ **Allspice:**
Ground: Use in baking, puddings, relishes, some jellies and preserves.

♥ **Allspice:**
Whole: Use in pickling, meats, gravies and to boil fish.

♥ **Aniseed:**
Use in cookies, candies, sweet pickles, on coffee cakes, sweet rolls.

♥ **Basil:**
Use in tomato dishes, on peas, squash, green beans.

♥ **Bay Leaves:**
Use in pickling, stews, tomato aspic, soups.

♥ **Caraway Seeds:**
Use in rye bread, rolls, sauerkraut, new cabbage, noodle dishes.

♥ **Cardamom Seeds:**
Use in sweet rolls, breads, coffee cakes, beverages.

♥ **Cinnamon, Ground:**
Use in pies, cookies, cakes, puddings, desserts, sweet potatoes, on coffee cakes and sweet rolls.

♥ **Cinnamon, Stick:**
Use in pickling and preserving. For flavoring puddings and stewed fruits.

♥ **Cayenne:**
Use in meats, fish, sauces, relishes, oyster stew, egg dishes.

♥ **Celery Seeds:**
Use in pickling, fish, salads, salad dressings.

SPICES & HOW TO USE THEM

♥ **Chervil:**
Use in soups, salads, egg dishes, fish sauces. Use in meats, cocktail sauces and vegetables.

♥ **Chili Powder:**
Use in meats, cocktail sauces and vegetables.

♥ **Cloves, Ground:**
Use in cookies, cakes, pies, puddings, stews, vegetables.

♥ **Cloves, Whole:**
Use in pork and ham roasts, pickling of fruit, spiced sweet syrups.

♥ **Curry Powder:**
Use in sauces for vegetables, eggs, fish, seafood and meat.

♥ **Dill Seeds:**
Use in pickling, sauerkraut, salads, soups, fish and meat sauces, gravies, spiced vinegar.

♥ **Fennel Seeds:**
Use in sweet pickles, boiled fish, pastries, pickling, and in cooked dried fruits, apple sauce.

♥ **Ginger, Ground:**
Use in gingerbread, cakes, pumpkin pie.

♥ **Ginger, Cracked:**
Puddings, canned fruits, pot roasts and other meats.

♥ **Laurel Leaves:**
Use in beef stews, pot roast, chowder, beets and pickles.

♥ **Mace, Ground:**
Use in pound cakes and chocolate dishes.

♥ **Mace, Whole:**
Use in fish sauces, pickling, stewed cherries.

♥ **Marjoram:**
Use in stews, soups, tomato juice, cottage cheese, stuffings, fish, fish sauces.

171

♥ **Mixed Pickling Spice:**
Use in pickling and preserving of meats, vegetables, relishes, gravies, sauces, stews.

♥ **Mustard Seed, Whole:**
To garnish salads, pickled meats, fish, hamburgers.

♥ **Mustard, Dry:**
Use in meats, sauces, gravies, baked beans, lima beans, casseroles.

♥ **Nutmeg, Ground:**
Use in pies, cakes, cookies, sauces, puddings and as topping for eggnog, on cauliflower, spinach.

♥ **Nutmeg, Whole:**
Use in dishes above, after grating.

♥ **Oregano:**
Use in meat dishes, sauces, gravies, omelets.

♥ **Paprika:**
Use in meat, poultry and fish dishes, salad dressings. Use on fish, shellfish, salad, vegetables, canapés.

♥ **Pepper, Ground:**
Use in meats, sauces, gravies, vegetables, soups, salads, eggs, etc.

♥ **Pepper, Whole:**
Use in pickling, soups and meats.

♥ **Poppy Seed:**
Use as a topping for bread, rolls, cookies. Good in salads, noodles, fillings for pastries.

♥ **Rosemary:**
Use in lamb dishes, soups, stews and in fish and meat stocks.

♥ **Saffron:**
Use in baked goods and chicken, fish and rice dishes.

♥ **Sage:**
Use in stuffings for meat, fish and poultry, meat sauces and gravies.

SPICES & HOW TO USE THEM

♥ **Savory:**
Use in meats, chicken, stuffings, fish sauces.

♥ **Sesame Seed:**
Use in sauces, salads, soups, tomato dishes.

♥ **Thyme:**
Use in stews, chowders, poultry stuffings and meat and fish sauces.

♥ **Turmeric:**
Used in combination with mustard for pickling.

Containers

♥ 1 c. = 8 oz. can

♥ 1 3/4 c. = #300 can

♥ 2 c. = #303 can

♥ 2 1/2 c. = # 2 can

♥ 3 1/2 c. = # 2 1/2 can

♥ 6 1/2 to 6 3/4 c. = #10 can

Equivalents

♥ 3 tsp. = 1 Tbs.

♥ 4 Tbs. = 1/4 c.

♥ 5 1/3 Tbs. = 1/3 c.

♥ 8 Tbs. = 1/2 c.

♥ 10 2/3 Tbs. = 2/3 c.

♥ 12 Tbs. = 3/4 c.

♥ 16 Tbs. = 1 c.

♥ 1/2 c. = 1 gill

♥ 2 c. = 1 pint

♥ 4 c. = 1 quart

♥ 4 quarts = 1 gallon

♥ 8 quarts = 1 peck

♥ 4 pecks = 1 bushel

♥ 16 oz. = 1 pound

♥ 32 oz. = 1 quart

♥ 8 oz. liquid = 1 c.

♥ 1 oz. liquid = 2 Tbs.

♥ A leaf of lettuce dropped into the pot absorbs the grease from the top of the soup. Remove the lettuce and throw it away as soon as it has served its purpose.

♥ To prevent splashing when frying meat, sprinkle a little salt into the pan before putting the oil in.

♥ Small amounts of leftover corn may be added to pancake batter for variety. To make bread crumbs, use fine cutter of the food grinder and tie a large paper bag over the spout to prevent flying crumbs.

♥ When bread is baking, a small dish of water in the oven will help keep the crust from getting hard.

♥ Rinse a pan in cold water before scalding milk to prevent sticking.

♥ When you are creaming butter and sugar together, it's a good idea to rinse the bowl with boiling water first. They will cream faster.

♥ To melt chocolate, grease pan in which it is to be melted.

♥ Dip the spoon in hot water to measure shortening, butter, etc. The fat will slip out more easily.

♥ When you buy cellophane wrapped cupcakes and notice that the cellophane is somewhat stuck to the frosting, hold the package under the cold water tap for a moment before you unwrap it. The cellophane will then come off clean.

♥ When you are doing any sort of baking, you get better results if you remember to preheat your cookie sheet, muffin tins, or cake pans.

♥ Chill cheese to grate it more easily.

♥ The odor from baking or boiling salmon may be eliminated by squeezing lemon juice on both sides of each salmon steak or on the cut surface of the salmon and letting it stand in the refrigerator for one hour or longer before cooking.

♥ Use the type of can opener that leaves a smooth edge and remove both ends from flat can (the size that tuna is usually packed in) and you have a perfect mold for poached eggs.

175

KITCHEN HELPS

♥ A clean clothespin provides a cool handle to steady the cake tin when removing a hot cake.

♥ Try using a thread instead of a knife when a cake is to be cut while it is hot.

♥ Potatoes soaked in salt water for 20 minutes before baking will bake more rapidly.

♥ Sweet potatoes will not turn dark if put in salted water (five teaspoons to one quart of water) immediately after peeling.

♥ Let raw potatoes stand in cold water for at least half an hour before frying to improve the crispness of french fried potatoes.

♥ Use a strawberry huller to peel potatoes which have been boiled in their "jackets".

♥ Use greased muffin tins as molds when baking stuffed green peppers.

♥ A few drops of lemon juice in the water will whiten boiled potatoes.

♥ The skins will remain tender if you wrap potatoes in aluminum foil to bake them. They are attractively served in the foil, too.

♥ If you add a little milk to water in which cauliflower is cooking, the cauliflower will remain white.

♥ When cooking cabbage, place a small tin cup or can half full of vinegar on the stove near the cabbage, and it will absorb all odor from it.

♥ It is important when and how you add salt to cooking. To blend with soups and sauces, put it in early, but add it to meats just before taking from the stove. In cake ingredients, salt can be mixed with the eggs. When cooking vegetables always salt the water in which they are cooked. Put salt in the pan when frying fish.

176

KITCHEN HELPS

♥ It is easy to remove the white membrane from oranges for fancy desserts or salads by soaking them in boiling water for five minutes before you peel them.

♥ You can get more juice from a dried up lemon if you heat it for five minutes in boiling water before you squeeze it.

♥ If it's important to you to get walnut meats out whole, soak the nuts overnight in salt water before you crack them.

♥ If the whipping cream looks as though it's not going to whip, add three or four drops of lemon juice or a bit of plain gelatin powder to it and it probably will.

♥ For quick and handy seasoning while cooking, keep on hand a large shaker containing six parts of salt and one of pepper.

♥ Dip your bananas in lemon juice right after they are peeled. They will not turn dark and the faint flavor of lemon really adds quite a bit. The same may be done with apples.

♥ To preserve leftover egg yolk for future use, place them into a small bowl and add two tablespoons of salad oil. Then put into refrigerator. The egg yolks will remain soft and fresh, and egg yolks kept in this way can be used many ways.

♥ You may determine the age of an egg by placing it in the bottom of a bowl of cold water. If it lays on its side, it is strictly fresh, if it stands at an angle it is at least three days old and ten days old if stands on end.

♥ To keep egg yolks from crumbling when slicing hard cooked eggs, wet the knife before each cut.

♥ Bread crumbs added to scrambled eggs will improve the flavor and make larger helpings possible.

♥ A tablespoon of vinegar added to the water when poaching eggs will help set the whites so they will not spread.

♥ When cooking eggs it helps prevent cracking if you wet the shells in cold water before placing them in boiling water.

177

KITCHEN HELPS

♥ Add a little vinegar to the water when an egg cracks during boiling. It will help seal the egg.

♥ Meringue will not shrink if you spread it on the pie so that it touches the crust on each side and bake it in a moderate oven.

♥ When you cook eggs in the shell, put a big teaspoon of salt in the water. Then the shells won't crack.

♥ Set eggs in a pan of warm water before using as this releases all whites from shells.

♥ Egg whites for meringue should be set out to room temperature before beating, then they can be beaten to greater volume.

♥ If you want to make a pecan pie and haven't any nuts, substitute crushed cornflakes. They will rise to the top the same as nuts and give a delicious flavor and crunchy surface.

♥ To prevent crust from becoming soggy with cream pie, sprinkle crust with powdered sugar.

♥ Cut drinking straws into short lengths and insert through slits in pie crusts to prevent juice from running over in the oven and to permit steam to escape.

♥ Put a layer of marshmallows in the bottom of a pumpkin pie, then add the filling. You will have a nice topping as the marshmallows will come to the top.

♥ If the juice from your apple pie runs over in the oven, shake some salt on it, which causes the juice to burn to a crisp so it can be removed.

♥ Use cooking or salad oil in waffles and hot cakes in the place of shortening. No extra pan or bowl to melt shortening and no waiting.

♥ A pie crust will be more easily made and better if all the ingredients are cool.

♥ The lower pie crust should be placed in the pan so that it covers the surface smoothly. Be sure no air lurks beneath the surface, for it will push the crust out of shape in baking.

178

♥ Folding the top crust over the lower crust before crimping will keep the juices in the pie.

♥ In making custard type pies, bake at a high temperature for about ten minutes to prevent soggy crust. Then finish baking at a lower temperature.

♥ Fill cake pans about two-thirds full and spread batter well into corners and to the sides, leaving a slight hollow in the center.

♥ The cake is done when it shrinks slightly from the sides of the pan or if it springs back when touched lightly with the finger.

♥ After a cake comes from the oven, it should be placed on a rack for about five minutes. Then the sides should be loosened and the cake turned out on rack to finish cooling.

♥ Kneading the dough for a half minute after mixing improves the texture of baking powder biscuits.

♥ Use crushed potato chips instead of bread crumbs for meat loaf filler. The flavor is delicious.

♥ If your meat loaf is too greasy, put a slice of bread in the bottom of the pan. The bread soaks up the extra grease.

♥ To keep bacon from splattering or shrinking, coat by shaking in a bag of flour and fry.

♥ For hamburgers to cook in a hurry, poke a hole in the center, it disappears when cooked.

♥ When a flavor change is wanted, use potato flakes or crushed cereal to thicken stews and sauces.

♥ Use a small amount of baking powder in your gravy if it seems quite greasy; the grease will disappear.

♥ To scald milk without scorching, add a tiny amount of sugar and do not stir.

♥ If a recipe calls for buttermilk or sour milk, you may substitute by adding a teaspoon of vinegar to a cup of fresh milk.

The one thing harder than sticking to a diet is keeping quiet about it.

Index of Recipes

He did good, and gave us rain from heaven, and fruitful seasons, filling our hearts with food and gladness. Acts 14:17b

INDEX OF RECIPES

INDEX OF RECIPES

INDEX OF RECIPES

FROSTINGS

PIES

COOKIES

CANDY

MISCELLANEOUS

Table Of Contents

ISBN:
13: 978-0-9792562-0-2
10: 0-9792562-0-8

Note of Appreciation:

*In my travels as a preacher's wife it has been
our privilege to feast at the table of some wonderful
Christian ladies. The delicious meals have been
deeply appreciated and also the willingness of
these great cooks to share their recipes with me.
It's with this appreciation that we pass the
following recipes on to others, hoping you
will enjoy them as much as I have.*

Mrs. Mary Fellure

To order additional copies please visit our website @
www.victorybaptistpress.com